HOCKEY DRILL BOOK

This book is dedicated to the memory of my father, James Michael, who understood the real value of youth hockey – participation.

HOCKEY DRILL BOOK

Michael A. Smith

FIREFLY BOOKS

A FIREFLY BOOK

Second printing 1998.

We acknowledge the financial support of the Government of Canada through the Book Publishing Industry Development Program for our publishing activities.

Cataloguing in Publication Data

Smith, Michael A.
    The hockey drill book

Includes index.
ISBN 1-55209-066-3

1. Hockey - Training. 2. Hockey - Coaching. I. Title

GV848.3.S65 1996   796.962'2 C96-930946-5

Published by
Firefly Books Ltd.
3680 Victoria Park Avenue
Willowdale, Ontario
Canada M2H 3K1

Published in the U.S. by
Firefly Books (U.S.) Inc.
P.O. Box 1338, Ellicott Station
Buffalo, New York 14205

Book Design: Fortunato Aglialoro
Falcom Design & Communications Inc.

Printed and bound in Canada by
Friesens
Altona, Manitoba

CONTENTS

"Just give me a group of gentlemen, who play the game hard but clean, and always on an upward path. Then the championships will take care of themselves if the overall ability of the team warrants them."

John Wooden
They Call Me Coach

INTRODUCTION

Training sessions, more commonly called practices, formulate an important part of hockey. Success of a team, whether it is measured an Improvement, winning, or fun is directly dependent on practices. The better the practices, the better the team. What goes into a practice, how a practice is conducted, and what is accomplished during a practice is critical. In this sense, the drills that practices are comprised of are essential to the development of the team.

This book presents 200 drills in eight different chapters: skating, stickhandling, passing, shooting, conditioning, goaltending, checking and situations. The book attempts to present a comprehensive selection of drills. Drills for the different levels of competition and for different stages of development are shown. It is hoped that the book will serve all coaches whether it be as a readily available drill reminder or source for new and different drills.

The method of the book is to provide a diagram for each drill, its purpose, a brief description, the number of participation, and the tempo of the drill's execution. Many of the drills have variations listed as well.

No drill is too simple to be used. Drills are the methods that the fundamental skills of the game are taught. All teams should constantly be practicing these fundamentals. As a team develops its skills, the drills can become more complex. Teams should, at some time, begin to use drills that combine a number of skills.

The most important thing to consider in drill selection for the coach is to keep in mind that the drill should be fun. Fun, not in the sense of being relaxing and humorous, but in the sense that it is substantial, worthwhile, and enjoyable. Good drills make coaching and playing a good experience.

KEY TO SYMBOLS

SYMBOL	DESCRIPTION
(S)	Starting point
▲	Pylon
◀———	Skater, arrow shows direction of movement
---▶----	Skater with puck, arrow shows direction of movement
·······▶········	Pass, arrow shows direction
·—–◀—–	Shot on goal
⌒	Jump (over line or pylon)
∿∿∿∿∿∿	Skate backwards
xxxxxxxxxxx	Cross-over forwards
‖	Full stop

CHAPTER 1

Skating

"...the main thing in the tactics of this game was to be able to constantly create numerical superiority in every spot on the ice where the puck is, and in order to achieve this, they had to skate as they never skated before, wide open."

Anatoli Tarasov
The Road to Olympus

Drill 1. *Warm-up 1*

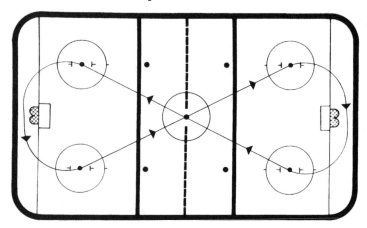

Purpose:
To provide a warm-up at the start of practice and to improve body movements while skating.

Description:
Performed while skating Figure 8's. A variety of body exercises are done to allow the players to stretch. The coach (or a player) can call out the exercises. Suggested exercises: knee bends, squats, body twists, run on toes, jumps, knee drops, full body drops, 180 and 360 degree spins.

Tempo:
Drill is started at a slow speed and increased during execution.

Participation:
The entire team.

Variations:
Performed while skating laps; performed in three (3) groups, one (1) group in each zone.

Drill 2. *Warm-up 2*

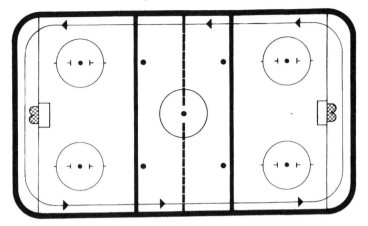

Purpose:
To provide a warm-up at the start of practice and to improve the player's dexterity with the stick.

Description:
Performed while skating laps. A variety of exercises focused on the stick are done to allow the players to stretch. The coach (or a player) can call out the exercises. Suggested exercises: rotate sticks with wrists, rotate at the hips with the stick behind the back, windmill type movement with stick behind the neck, swing stick overhead with both hands on the stick, touch the toes with both hands on the stick, bend forward keeping knees stiff with the stick behind the back, and bend forward touching the stick to the heels with stick behind the legs.

Tempo:
Drill is started at slow speed and increased during execution.

Participation:
The entire team.

Variations:
Performed while skating Figure 8's; performed in three (3) groups, one (1) group in each zone.

Drill 3. *Warm-up 3*

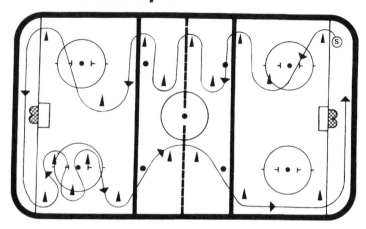

Purpose:
To provide a warm-up at the start of practice and to improve the player's skating ability.

Description:
Performed while skating laps. The players skate through a course laid out with obstacles. The obstacles are located to make the players execute short and long strides and tight and wide turns.

Tempo:
Drill is started at a slow speed and increased during execution.

Participation:
The entire team.

Variations:
Performed while skating backwards; performed alternating forward and backward skating; performed in time intervals, i.e., fast 10 seconds, slow 5 seconds; change the pattern of the obstacles.

Drill 4. *Stops 1*

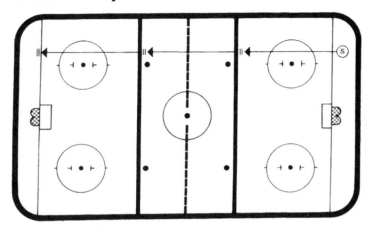

Purpose:
To provide a drill to practice stops.

Description:
Performed with players skating length of ice stopping at the two blue lines and the far goal line. Players should face the same way to insure that stops both ways are practiced.

Tempo:
Drill is executed from 3/4 to full speed.

Participation:
Team is divided into three (3) or four (4) groups. Drill is performed in groups. The second group starts after the first group has completed the first stop at the near blue line.

Variations:
Performed while skating backwards; performed alternating forward and backward skating.

Drill 5. *Stops 2*

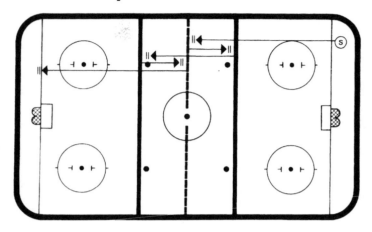

Purpose:
To provide a drill to practice stops and change of directions.

Description:
Players skate the length of ice in a predetermined pattern. One pattern is: to the red line, to the near blue line, to the far blue line, to the red line, to the far goal line. Players should face the same way to insure that stops both ways are practiced.

Tempo:
Drill is executed from 3/4 to full speed.

Participation:
Team is divided into three (3) or four (4) groups. Drill is performed in groups. The second group starts after the first group has executed the second stop (near blue line).

Variations:
Performed while skating backwards; performed alternating forward and backward skating; performed with different patterns, i.e., to the far blue line, to the near blue line, to the far blue line.

Drill 6. *Stops 3*

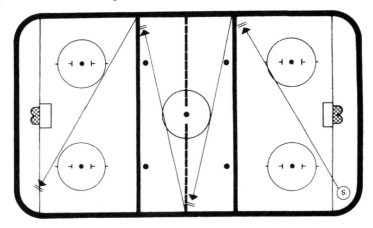

Purpose:

To provide a drill to practice stops and a change of directions.

Description:

Players skate a diagonal pattern stopping where the blue lines, red line and goal lines meet the boards. This is a good drill to practice one leg or partial stops. The players should face the same way to insure that stops both ways are practiced.

Tempo:

Drill is executed from 3/4 to full speed.

Participation:

The entire team with one player right after another.

Variations:

Performed while skating backwards; performed alternating forward and backward skating; team is divided into two (2) groups with each starting in opposite corners at the same end.

Drill 7. *Stops 4*

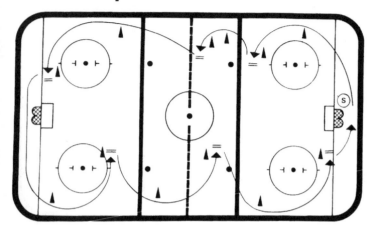

Purpose:
To provide a drill to practice stops while making turns.

Description:
Players skate in a course laid out with obstacles. The stops are executed at every second obstacle. The stops teach the players to stop during and after turns. The players should face the same way to insure that stops both ways are executed.

Tempo:
Drill is executed at 3/4 to full speed.

Participation:
The entire team with one player right after another.

Variations:
Performed while skating backwards; performed alternating forward and backward skating; obstacles are changed to alter the pattern.

Drill 8. *Stops 5*

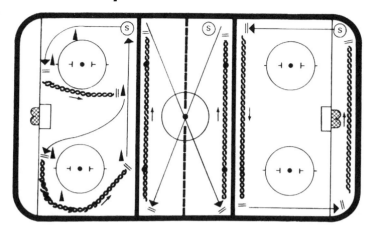

Purpose:
To provide a drill combining forward and backward stops.

Description:
Players skate in three (3) different patterns, one in each zone. The drills teach the players to stop while skating forward and backward in different situations.

Tempo:
Drill is executed from 3/4 to full speed.

Participation:
Team is divided into three (3) groups, one (1) in each zone. The groups rotate through each zone.

Variations:
Change the patterns in each zone.

Drill 9. *Stops 6*

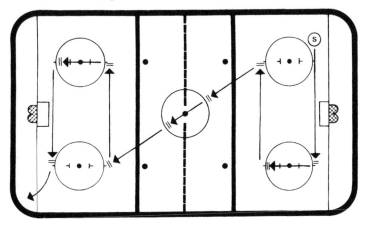

Purpose:
To provide a drill to practice stops.

Description:
Players skate in a predetermined pattern using the face-off circles. The pattern enables the players to practice stops while executing both long and short strides.

Tempo:
Drill is executed from 3/4 to full speed.

Participation:
The entire team with one player right after another.

Variations:
Change the pattern.

Drill 10. *Stepovers 1*

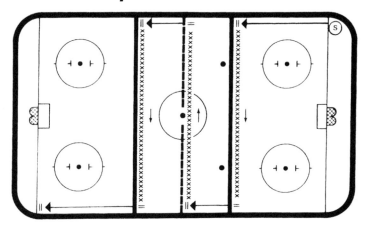

Purpose:
To provide a drill to practice stepovers.

Description:
Performed along the blue lines and red line. The coach must be sure the stepovers are executed properly. This is a good drill to find out which players have problems executing the stepovers. The players should always face the same end to insure that stepovers both ways are practiced.

Tempo:
Drill is executed at a normal speed relative to each group. If the drill is done too quickly, many players will not execute properly.

Participation:
The entire team with one player right after another.

Drill 11. *Stepovers 2*

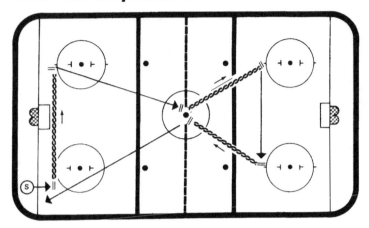

Purpose:

To provide a drill that combines stepovers with forward and backward skating.

Description:

Players execute stepovers in a predetermined pattern laid out with the face-off circles. This drill provides the opportunity to execute forward and backward turns as well. The coach must be sure the stepovers are executed properly.

Tempo:

Drill is executed at a normal speed relative to each group. If the drill is done too quickly, many players will not execute properly.

Participation:

The entire team with one player right after another.

Variations:

Change the pattern.

Drill 12. *Stepovers 3*

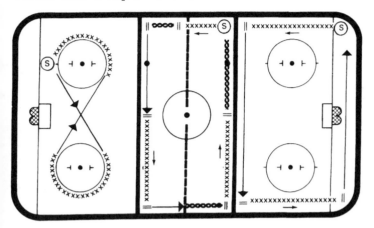

Purpose:
To provide a drill that combines stepovers with forward and backward skating.

Description:
Players execute stepovers in three (3) different patterns, one (1) in each zone. This drill combines forward and backward skating with stepovers. The coach must be sure the stepovers are executed properly.

Tempo:
Drill is executed at a normal speed relative to each group. If the drill is executed at a speed too quick, many players will not execute properly.

Participation:
The team is divided into three (3) groups, one (1) in each zone. The groups rotate through each zone.

Variations:
Change the patterns in each zone.

Drill 13. *Crossovers 1*

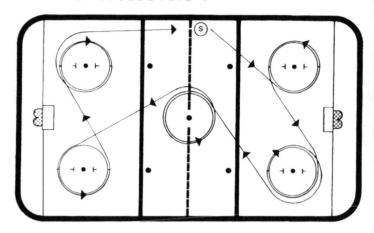

Purpose:
To provide a drill to practice crossovers.

Description:
Players skate around each of the five (5) face-off circles. This enables the players to practice crossovers both to the left and to the right.

Tempo:
Drill is executed from 3/4 to full speed.

Participation:
Team is divided into groups of three (3) to five (5) players. The second group starts when the first group has completed its crossovers at the second face-off circle.

Variations:
Performed while skating backwards; performed alternating forward and backward skating.

Drill 14. *Crossovers 2*

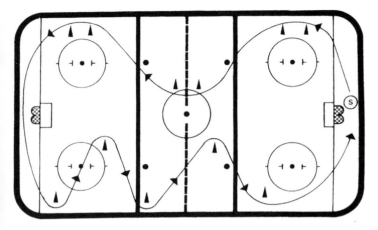

Purpose:
To provide a drill to practice crossovers.

Description:
The players skate a predetermined pattern laid out with obstacles. The players practice both wide and tight crossovers.

Tempo:
Drill is executed from 3/4 to full speed.

Participation:
The entire team with one player right after another.

Variations:
Performed while skating backwards; performed alternating forward and backward skating; change the patterns.

Drill 15. *Crossovers 3*

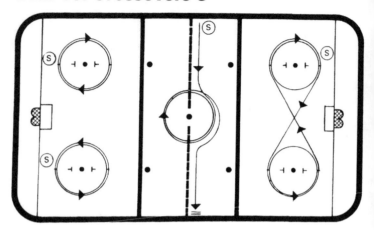

Purpose:
To provide a drill to practice crossovers.

Description:
Players skate three (3) predetermined patterns, one (1) in each zone. This drill emphasizes tight crossovers.

Tempo:
Drill is executed from 3/4 to full speed.

Participation:
Team is divided into three (3) groups, one (1) to each zone. The groups rotate through each zone.

Variations:
Performed while skating backwards; performed alternating forward and backward skating.

Drill 16. *Crossovers 4*

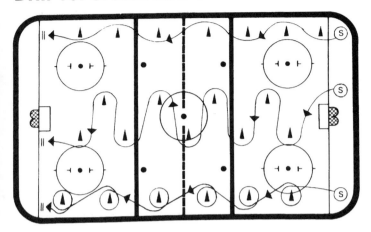

Purpose:
To provide a drill to practice crossovers.

Description:
Players skate three (3) predetermined patterns laid out with obstacles. The patterns allow wide and tight crossovers to be executed.

Tempo:
Drill is executed from 3/4 to full speed.

Participation:
Team is divided into three (3) groups, one (1) for each pattern. The groups rotate through each pattern.

Variations:
Performed while skating backwards; change the patterns.

Drill 17. *Stops and Crossovers 1*

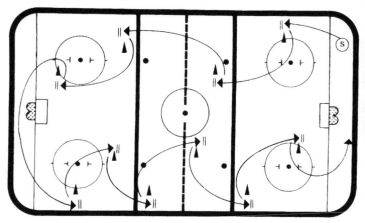

Purpose:
To provide a drill that combines stops and crossovers.

Description:
Players skate a pattern laid out with obstacles. The players execute crossovers both to the left and right. The crossovers are executed after the stops.

Tempo:
Drill is executed from 3/4 to full speed.

Participation:
The entire team with one player right after another.

Variations:
Performed while skating backwards; performed alternating forward and backward skating; change the pattern.

Drill 18. *Stops and Crossovers 2*

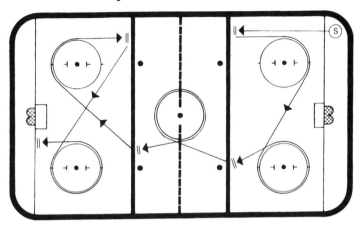

Purpose:
To provide a drill that combines stops and crossovers.

Description:
Players skate a pattern that is laid out with the face-off circles. The players execute crossovers and stops both to the left and right.

Tempo:
Drill is executed from 3/4 to full speed.

Participation:
The entire team with one player right after another.

Variations:
Performed while skating backwards; performed alternating forward and backward skating.

Drill 19. *Balance 1*

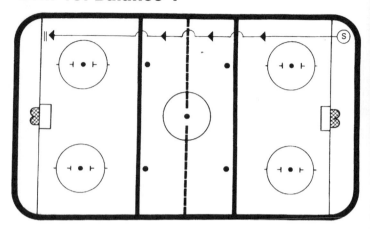

Purpose:
To provide a drill that practices jumps.

Description:
Players skate length of ice executing jumps at the blue lines and the red line.

Tempo:
Drill is executed at a normal speed relative to each group. If the drill is executed at a speed too quick, many players will not execute the jumps properly.

Participation:
Team is divided into groups of three (3) to five (5) players. The second group starts when the first group has completed its first jump.

Variations:
Performed while skating backwards.

Drill 20. *Balance 2*

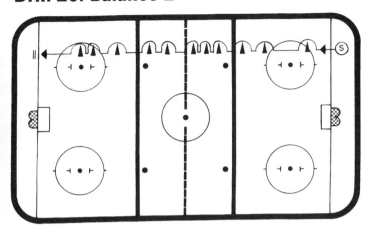

Purpose:
To provide a drill that practices jumps.

Description:
Players skate length of ice executing jumps over the obstacles. The obstacles are laid in a manner that enables the players to jump from both short and long strides.

Tempo:
Drill is executed at a normal speed relative to each group. If the drill is executed at a speed too quick, many players will not execute the jumps properly.

Participation:
The entire team, one player right after another.

Variations:
Change the pattern.

Drill 21. *Balance 3*

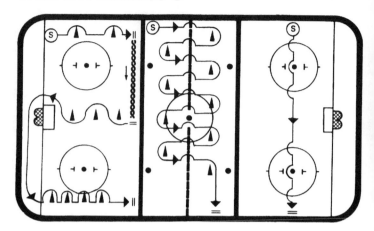

Purpose:
To provide a drill that practices jumps.

Description:
The players skate three (3) patterns, one (1) in each zone. This drill combines crossovers with forward and backward skating with jumps.

Tempo:
Drill is executed at a normal speed relative to each group. If the drill is executed at a speed too quick, many players will not execute the jumps properly.

Participation:
Team is divided into three (3) groups, one (1) in each zone. The groups rotate through each zone.

Variations:
Change the patterns in each zone.

Drill 22. *Balance 4*

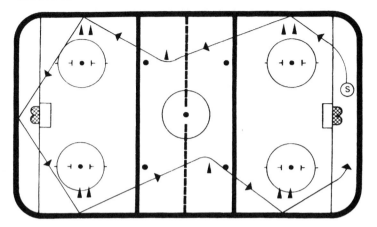

Purpose:

To provide a drill that teaches the players to maintain their balance after contact with the boards.

Description:

Performed while skating laps. The players make contact at the designated spots. This is executed in a manner that has the player throw his body against the boards while skating.

Tempo:

Drill is executed at a normal speed relative to each group. If the drill is executed at a speed too quick, the players will not maintain their balance after the contact.

Participation:

The entire team with one player right after another.

Drill 23. *Breakout*

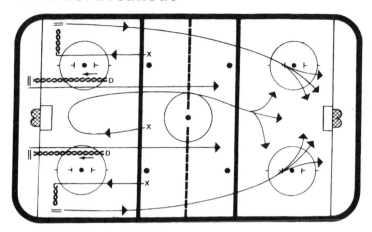

Purpose:
To provide a drill that simulates the skating patterns of the team's breakout system.

Description:
The players execute the positional skating patterns of the team's breakout system. The players should interchange with the different positions to be familiar with the different patterns.

Tempo:
Drill is executed from 3/4 to full speed.

Participation:
Team is divided into five (5) man units. Drill can also be executed with just the forwards or defensemen.

Drill 24. *Defensive System*

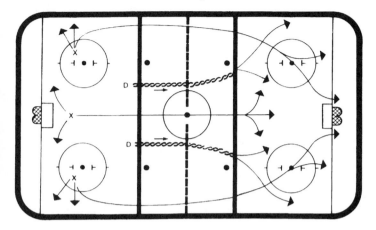

Purpose:

To provide a drill that simulates the skating patterns of the team's defensive system.

Description:

The players execute the positional skating patterns of the team's defensive system. The players should interchange the different positions to be familiar with the different patterns.

Tempo:

Drill is executed from 3/4 to full speed.

Participation:

Team is divided into five (5) man units. Drill can also be performed with just the forwards or defensemen.

Drill 25. *Obstacle Course*

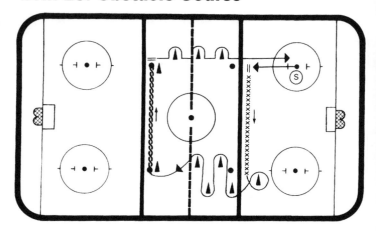

Purpose:
To provide a drill that practices the different skating skills.

Description:
An obstacle course is laid out. The players skate the course executing the different skills. It should include forward and backward skating, crossovers, stepovers, jumps, stops. Time trials make it competitive and is a method to evaluate improvement.

Tempo:
Drill is executed at full speed.

Participation:
The entire team. Drill may be executed one at a time or one player right after another.

Variations:
Change the course.

CHAPTER 2

Stickhandling

"When learning a movement, keep to the principle of going from the 'known to unknown', then you are sure to make progress."

Oleg Spassky
Ice Hockey

Drill 26. *Warm-up 1*

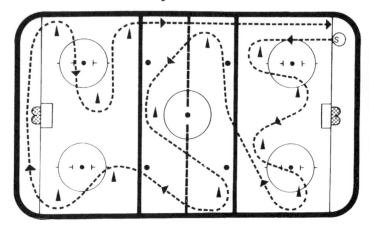

Purpose:

To provide a warm-up at the start of practice and to improve the player's ability to handle the puck.

Description:

Performed with the players skating a pattern laid out with obstacles. The pattern is such that the players make tight and wide turns while carrying the puck.

Tempo:

Drill is started at a slow speed and increased during execution.

Participation:

The entire team, one player right after another.

Variations:

Performed while skating backwards; change the pattern.

Drill 27. *Warm-up 2*

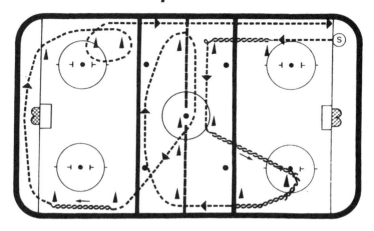

Purpose:
To provide a warm-up at the start of practice and to improve the player's ability to handle the puck.

Description:
Performed with the players skating a pattern laid out with obstacles. The pattern is such that the players work on change of directions and the transition between forward and backward skating while handling the puck.

Tempo:
Drill is started at a slow speed and increased slightly during execution.

Participation:
The entire team with one player right after another.

Variations:
Change the pattern; include stepovers by inserting them into a segment.

Drill 28. *Stationary Puckhandling*

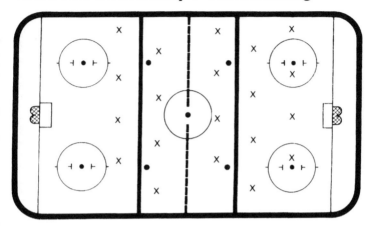

Purpose:

To provide a drill to practice the fundamentals of puckhandling.

Description:

Players are spread out over the ice. Start with the players stationary. Practice the basic fundamentals: regular dribble, short dribble, wide dribble, and quick dribble. Next, have the players make short movements (2-3 strides) to the left, right, forward, and backward. Dekes (against invisible opponents) should be practiced. Other things, such as dropping to one knee and both knees while stickhandling, can also be practiced.

Tempo:

Stationary, the movements begin at a slow speed and gradually increase.

Participation:

The entire team.

Drill 29. *Puckhandling and Turns 1*

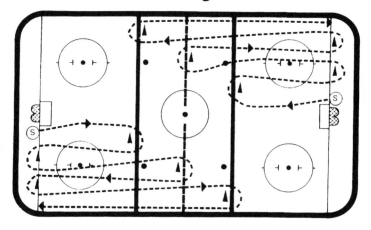

Purpose:
To provide a drill to practice turns while handling the puck.

Description:
Players skate forward to the near blue line, make a turn and return to the goal line. This is repeated to the red line and the far blue line. Obstacles are used for the turns.

Tempo:
Drill is executed from 3/4 to full speed.

Participation:
Team is divided into two (2) groups, one (1) at each end of the ice. The second player starts when the first reaches the near blue line.

Variations:
Performed skating backwards.

Drill 30. *Puckhandling and Turns 2*

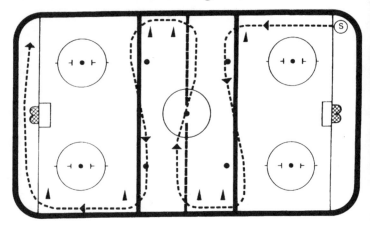

Purpose:
To provide a drill to practice turns while handling the puck.

Description:
Performed by skating along the two blue lines and the red lines. Obstacles are used as guides.

Tempo:
Drill is executed from 3/4 to full speed.

Participation:
The entire team with one player right after another.

Variations:
Performed skating backwards.

Drill 31. *Puckhandling and Turns 3*

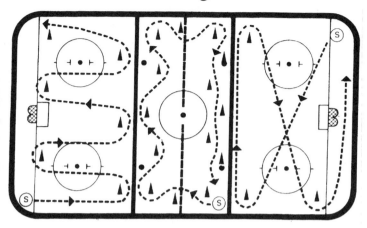

Purpose:
To provide a drill to practice turns while handling the puck.

Description:
Players skate in three (3) different patterns, one (1) in each zone. The patterns are laid out with obstacles. The patterns are such that both wide and tight turns are executed.

Tempo:
Drill is executed from 3/4 to full speed.

Participation:
Team is divided into three (3) groups, one (1) in each zone. The groups rotate through each zone.

Variations:
Performed while skating backwards; performed alternating forward and backward skating.

Drill 32. *Puckhandling and Circles 1*

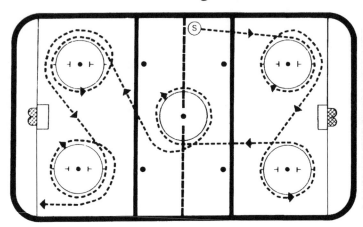

Purpose:
To provide a drill to practice crossovers while handling the puck.

Description:
Players skate around each of the five (5) face-off circles. This enables the players to practice crossovers to the left and right while handling the puck.

Tempo:
Drill is executed from 3/4 to full speed.

Participation:
Team is divided into groups of three (3) to five (5) players. The second group starts when the first group has completed its crossovers at the second face-off circle.

Variations:
Performed while skating backwards; performed alternating forward and backward skating.

Drill 33. *Puckhandling and Circles 2*

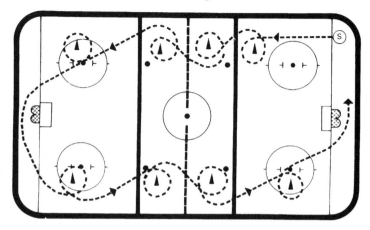

Purpose:
> To provide a drill to practice crossovers while handling the puck.

Description:
> Obstacles are laid out around the rink in a lap like fashion. Players skate around the rink executing tight circles around each of the obstacles.

Tempo:
> Drill is executed from 1/2 to full speed.

Participation:
> The entire team, the second player leaves after the first player has completed the first circle.

Variations:
> Performed while skating backwards; performed alternating forward and backward skating; the number of obstacles can be increased or decreased.

Drill 34. *Puckhandling and Turns 4*

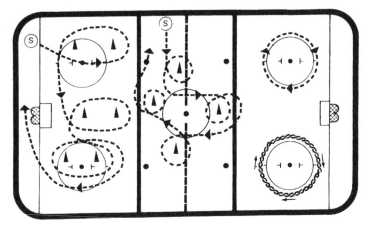

Purpose:
To provide a drill to practice crossovers while handling the puck.

Description:
Players skate three (3) different patterns, one (1) in each zone. The patterns are laid out with obstacles and the face-off circles. The patterns are such that both wide and tight crossovers are executed.

Tempo:
Drill is executed from 1/2 to full speed.

Participation:
is divided into three (3) groups, one (1) in each zone. The groups rotate through each zone.

Variations:
Performed while skating backwards; performed alternating forward and backward skating; change the patterns.

Drill 35. *Puckhandling and Stops 1*

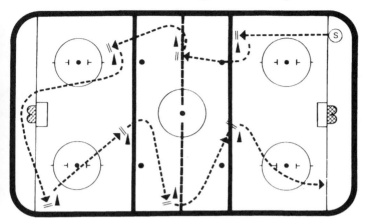

Purpose:
To provide a drill to practice stops while handling the puck.

Description:
Players skate a predetermined pattern laid out with obstacles. Full stops are executed at each obstacle. The coach must be sure players practice stops both ways.

Tempo:
Drill is executed from 3/4 to full speed.

Participation:
The entire team, the second player leaves after the first player has completed his first stop.

Variations:
Change the pattern.

Drill 36. *Puckhandling and Stops 2*

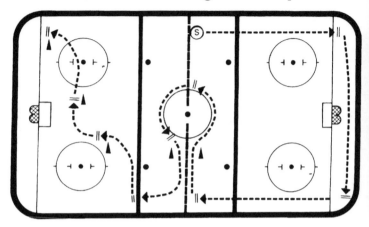

Purpose:
To provide a drill to practice stops while handling the puck.

Description:
Players skate a predetermined pattern laid out with obstacles, face-off circles, and the blue and red lines. Drill enables players to execute stops while handling the puck on a straight line, while making crossovers, and while making turns.

Tempo:
Drill is executed from 3/4 to full speed.

Participation:
The entire team, the second player leaves after the first player has completed his first stop.

Variations:
Change the patterns.

Drill 37. *Puckhandling and Stops 3*

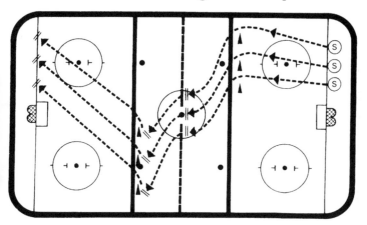

Purpose:
To provide a drill to practice stops while handling the puck.

Description:
Players skate the length of the ice executing turns and stops at the blue and red lines. Obstacles may be used.

Tempo:
Drill is executed at full speed.

Participation:
The team is divided into groups of three (3). The second group leaves after the first group passes the near blue line.

Variations:
Change the pattern.

Drill 38. *Puckhandling Medley*

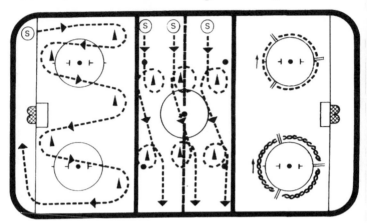

Purpose:

To provide a drill to practice various skating skills while handling the puck.

Description:

Players skate three (3) different patterns, one (1) in each zone. The patterns are laid out with the face-off circles and obstacles. Any number of skills can be practiced. In this example, turns, crossovers, and stops are used.

Tempo:

Drill is executed from 3/4 to full speed.

Participation:

Team is divided into three (3) groups, one (1) in each zone. The groups rotate through each zone.

Variations:

Performed skating backwards; performed alternating forward and backward skating; change the patterns; change the skating skills.

Drill 39. *Chaos 1*

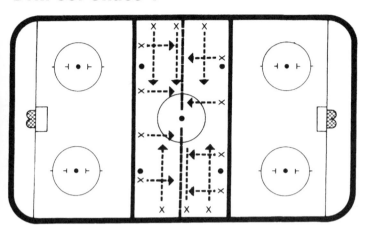

Purpose:

To provide a drill to train players to keep their heads up, maintain body control, and control the puck.

Description:

Players are divided into four (4) groups. Two (2) are lined up on opposite blue lines, and the other two are lined up on opposite boards at neutral ice. The groups skate simultaneously to the opposite side, with heads up and handling the puck. Players try to avoid contact while controlling the puck.

Tempo:

Drill is executed at 1/2 speed. To execute at a quicker tempo depends on the skill level of the players.

Participation:

The entire team, each group can hold up to six (6) to seven (7) players.

Drill 40. *Chaos 2*

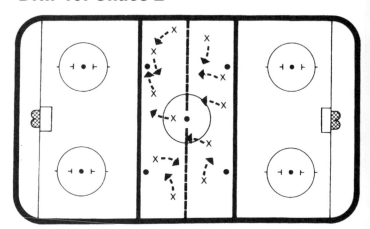

Purpose:
To provide a drill to train players to keep their heads up, maintain body control, and control the puck.

Description:
Players are confined to a limited area, in this drill the neutral zone. Each player has a puck. The players skate in all directions avoiding contact while handling the puck.

Tempo:
Drill is executed at 1/2 speed. To execute at a quicker tempo depends on the skill level of the players.

Participation:
The entire team. If smaller areas are used, fewer players may be used.

Variations:
Change the area size; insert a small number of players without a puck to try to knock the pucks away from the other players.

Drill 41. *Chaos 3*

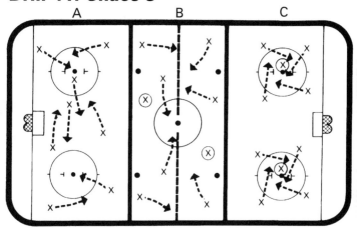

Purpose:
To provide a drill to train players to keep their heads up, maintain body control, and control the puck.

Description:
Three (3) different drills are executed, one (1) in each zone. The drills are: (A) Everyone with a puck; (B) A few players Ⓧ without pucks attempting to steal the pucks from the others; (C) One (1) player Ⓧ in face-off circle attempting to steal the puck from the others.

Tempo:
Drill is executed at 1/2 speed. To execute at a quicker tempo depends on the skill level of the players.

Participation:
Team is divided into three (3) groups, one (1) in each zone. The groups rotate through each zone.

Drill 42. *Dekes*

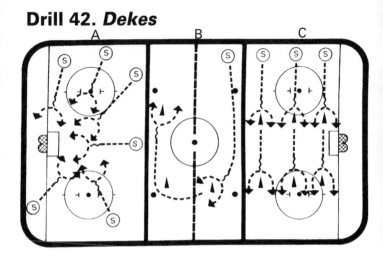

Purpose:

To provide a drill for the players with pucks to practice beating players without pucks (dekes).

Description:

Three (3) different drills are executed, one (1) in each zone. The drills are: (A) Players move toward the net making dekes; (B) Players make dekes at stationary objects; (C) Players make dekes at stationary objects.

Tempo:

Drill is executed from 1/2 to full speed.

Participation:

Team is divided into three (3) groups, one (1) in each zone. The groups rotate through each zone.

Variations:

Insert players without pucks to contest for the puck with the players with the pucks.

Drill 43. *2-0/1-1*

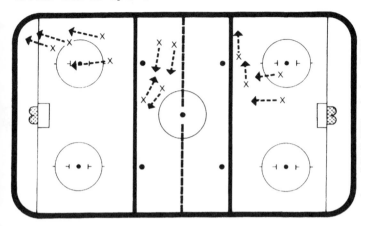

Purpose:
To provide a drill that makes puckhandling and deking competitive.

Description:
Players skate in pairs, each pair in a different direction, and with one puck per pair. At time intervals, players will skate 2-0 with one player handling the puck, then 1-1 with players contesting for control of the puck. *Note:* this is a good conditioning drill. For example, 10 seconds 2-0, 10 seconds 1-1, and 10 seconds rest.

Tempo:
Drill is executed at full speed.

Participation:
The entire team.

Variations:
Players can pass the puck during the 2-0 segment.

Drill 44. *Retrieve Pucks 1*

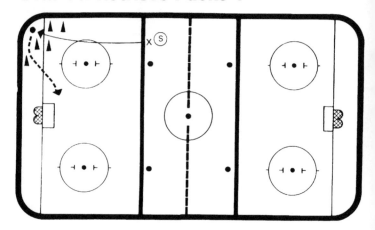

Purpose:

To provide a drill to teach players to gain control of the puck and carry it from the corner.

Description:

Obstacles are placed in the corner. A player will skate into the corner, gain control of the puck, and move from the corner. The obstacles force the player to execute skating skills while moving from the corner.

Tempo:

Drill is executed from 3/4 to full speed.

Participation:

Team can be divided up into as many as four (4) groups, one (1) to each corner.

Variations:

See Chapter 7 for checking drills.

Drill 45. *Retrieve Pucks 2*

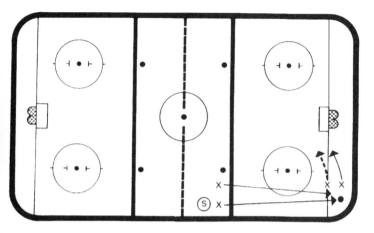

Purpose:

To provide a drill to teach players to gain control of the puck and carry it from the corner.

Description:

Two (2) players race to the corner. The first player takes control of the puck and must beat the second player to reach the net.

Tempo:

Drill is executed at full speed.

Participation:

Team can be divided up into as many as four (4) groups, one (1) to each corner.

Variations:

See Chapter 7 for checking drills.

Drill 46. *Retrieve Pucks 3*

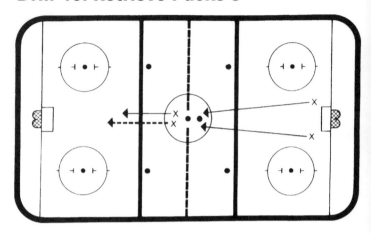

Purpose:
To provide a game type competitive drill.

Description:
Two (2) players race for a puck that is at center ice. The first player to the puck continues toward the net, and the second player attempts to prevent the first from getting there.

Tempo:
Drill is executed at full speed.

Participation:
The entire team, usually the winners continue to compete until there is a final winner.

Drill 47. *Chaos 4*

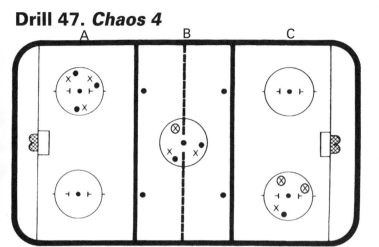

Purpose:
To provide a drill to train players to keep their heads up, maintain body control, and control the puck.

Description:
Three (3) different drills are executed using the face-off circles. The drills are: (A) Each player has a puck and they move in different directions; (B) Two (2) players have pucks and one Ⓧ player does not. The player without the puck attempts to steal the pucks from the others; (C) One (1) player has a puck and two (2) Ⓧ are without pucks. The players without pucks attempt to steal the puck from the other.

Tempo:
Drill is executed at 3/4 to full speed.

Participation:
Team is divided into groups of three (3). One (1) group is assigned to each circle.

Drill 48. *Puckhandling and the Feet 1*

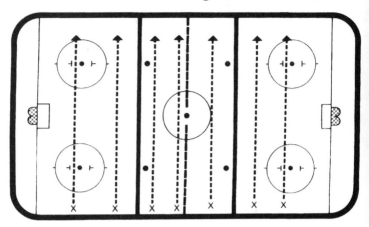

Purpose:

To teach players to control the puck with their feet.

Description:

Players, without sticks, skate across the ice and control
the puck with their feet.

Tempo:

Drill is executed at 1/2 speed. To execute at a quicker
tempo depends on the skill level of the players.

Participation:

The entire team.

Drill 49. *Puckhandling and the Feet 2*

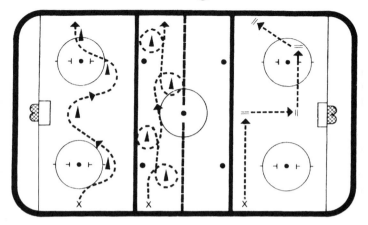

Purpose:
To teach players to control the puck with their feet.

Description:
Three (3) different patterns are laid out, one (1) in the red zone. The players execute each pattern by carrying the puck with their feet.

Tempo:
Drill is executed at 1/2 speed. To execute at a quicker tempo depends on the skill level of the players.

Participation:
The team is divided into three (3) groups, one (1) in each zone.

Drill 50. *Breakout*

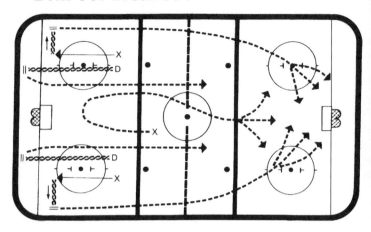

Purpose:

To provide a drill that simulates the puckhandling patterns of the team's breakout system.

Description:

The players execute the positional puckhandling patterns of the team's breakout system. Practice the players getting the puck at different places in the pattern. The players should interchange with the different positions to be familiar with the different patterns.

Tempo:

Drill is executed from 3/4 to full speed.

Participation:

Team is divided into five (5) man units. Drill can also be executed with just the forwards or the defensemen.

CHAPTER 3

Passing

"In order to receive or pass the puck in time, you must be well oriented in the play situation, see everything happening on the ice to foresee the immediate developments of the game...during training periods to dribble the puck without looking at it. Try to control the puck — not with your eyes, but with your stick. Keep your head high, watch your teammates and everything that is happening around you. And smile, make sure you smile. It is easier to master most intricate elements with a smile."

Nikolai Golomazov
Ice Hockey

Drill 51. *Stationary Passing*

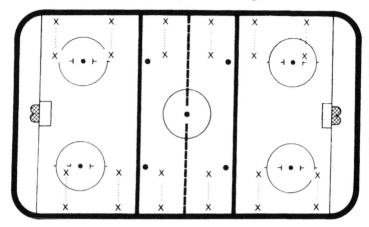

Purpose:

To provide a drill to practice the fundamentals of passing.

Description:

Players are spread out over the ice in pairs. Start with the players stationary. Practice the basic passes: wrist, snap, slap, lift, and backhand. Have the players take the passes on the forehand, backhand, and facing each other. Also vary the distances.

Tempo:

Begin with slow and easy passes and progress gradually to crisp passes.

Participation:

The entire team.

Drill 52. *Passes Making Laps*

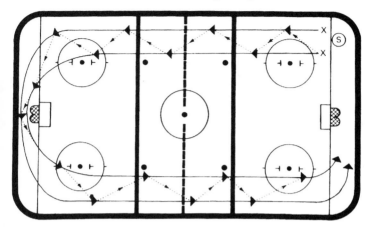

Purpose:
To provide a warm-up at the start of practice that utilizes passes.

Description:
Performed while skating laps. Players skate in pairs executing passes.

Tempo:
Drill is started at a slow speed and is increased during execution.

Participation:
The entire team.

Variation:
Players skate up the middle and turn, as a pair, to either side.

Drill 53. *Short Passes 1*

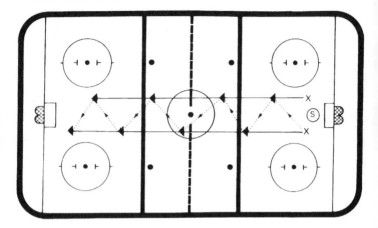

Purpose:

To provide a drill to teach short passes and one touch passes.

Description:

Players skate up the middle as a pair making short passes. Begin the drill with the players taking the pass and making a return pass after a couple of strides. Progress to one touch passing: receiving the pass and making the return pass are executed simultaneously.

Tempo:

Drill is started at a slow speed and is increased as the passing skill is improved.

Participation:

The entire team.

Variations:

Pairs go down the middle and back one side; pairs go down the middle and split up with one (1) player coming back on each side.

Drill 54. *Short Passes 2*

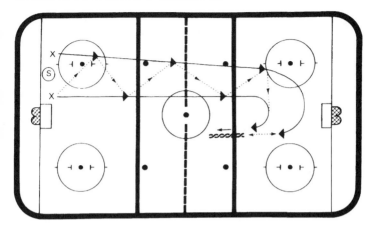

Purpose:
To provide a drill to teach short passes and one touch passes.

Description:
Players skate up the middle as a pair making short passes. The players come back with one skating backward and one skating forward making one touch passes.

Tempo:
Drill is started at a slow speed and is increased as the passing skill is improved.

Participation:
The entire team.

Drill 55. *Short Passes 3*

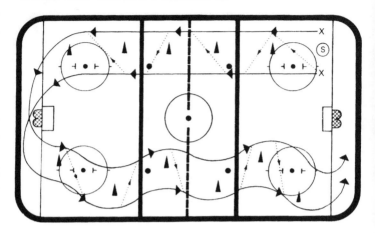

Purpose:
To provide a drill to teach short passes and one touch passes.

Description:
Obstacles are laid out along each side of the ice. Players skate laps in pairs passing between the obstacles. The players can either go in straight lines or in a weave pattern. Progress to one touch passes.

Tempo:
Drill is started at a slow speed and is increased as the passing skill is improved.

Participation:
The entire team.

Drill 56. *Short Passes 4*

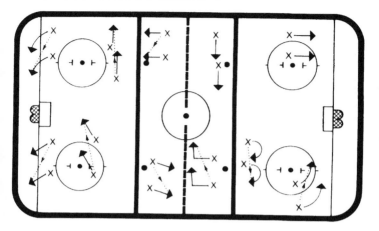

Purpose:
To provide a drill to teach short passes and one touch passes.

Description:
Players are spread around the ice in pairs. As pairs, players move in a confined area in all directions. Short and one touch passes are executed. This drill teaches anticipation.

Tempo:
Drill is executed from 3/4 to full speed.

Participation:
The entire team.

Drill 57. *Short Passes 5*

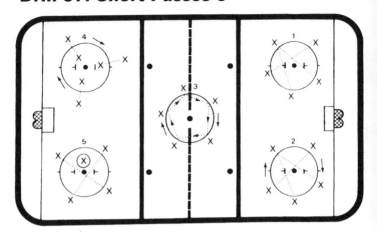

Purpose:

To provide a drill to teach short passes and one touch passes.

Description:

Five (5) different drills are executed, one (1) in each face-off circle. (1) Stationary diagonal passes; (2) Diagonal passes while moving; (3) Pass to player in front while moving; (4) Players skating in pairs around face-off circle; and (5) Man in middle ((X)) tries to intercept diagonal passes.

Tempo:

Drill is executed from 3/4 to full speed.

Participation:

Team is divided into five (5) groups, one (1) in each faceoff circle.

Drill 58. *Short Passes 6*

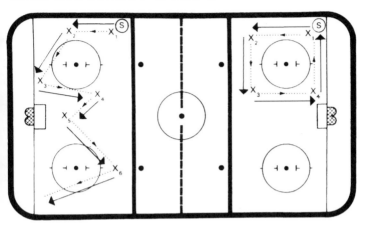

Purpose:

To provide a drill to teach short passes and one touch passes with player movement.

Description:

Players are aligned in groups of four (4) to six (6). Player makes pass and then follows the puck to that player. For example, X_1 passes to X_2 and X_1 moves to where X_2 is. X_2 passes to X_3 and moves to X_3.

Tempo:

Drill is executed from 3/4 to full speed.

Participation:

Team is divided into groups. The number and size of groups can vary. It is best to start with small groups and have the player movement be short. Increase the size of the group and distance as the passing skills improve.

Drill 59. *Short Passes 7*

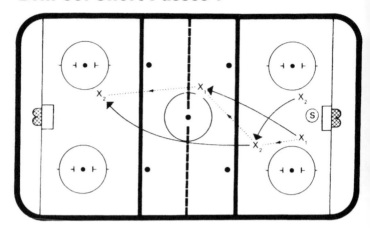

Purpose:

To provide a drill to teach short passes and one touch passes.

Description:

This drill teaches players, working in pairs, to head man the puck with short passes. The player making the pass breaks for an open spot for a return pass. For example, X_2 moves ahead of X_1 for a pass, X_1 moves ahead of X_2 for a pass and so on.

Tempo:

Drill is started at a slow speed and is increased as the passing skill is improved.

Participation:

The entire team.

Drill 60. *Short Passes 8*

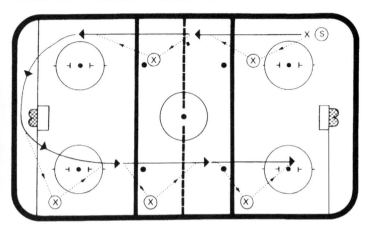

Purpose:
To provide a drill to teach short passes and one touch passes.

Description:
Players (X) skate around the ice in laps passing to other players Ⓧ who make return passes to X. Drill should progress until both X and Ⓧ make one touch passes.

Tempo:
Drill is executed from 3/4 to full speed.

Participation:
The entire team, second player leaves after first player makes his initial pass.

Variations:
Obstacles can be inserted to increase the difficulty.

Drill 61. *Long Passes 1*

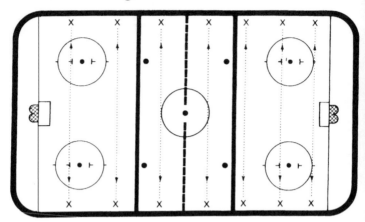

Purpose:
To provide a drill to teach long passes.

Description:
Players are lined up along the boards. Working in pairs, the basic fundamentals of long passes are practiced. Emphasis is placed on the *wrist* pass.

Tempo:
Begin with slow easy passes and progress to crisp passes.

Participation:
The entire team.

Variations:
Players can work in groups of four (4) and receive the pass from one player and pass to another.

Drill 62. *Long Passes 2*

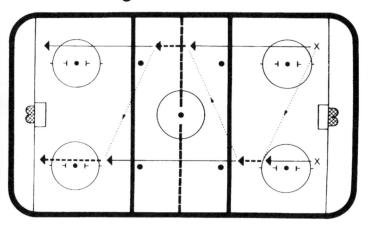

Purpose:

To provide a drill to teach long passes with player movement.

Description:

Players, working in pairs, skate the length of the ice. Each player stays wide to make the long passes.

Tempo:

Drill is started at a slow speed and is increased as the passing skill is improved.

Participation:

The entire team, second pair starts after first pair completes initial pass.

Variations:

Each player, skating up the ice, moves toward the middle after making the pass and returns toward the boards after receiving the pass. This results in a weave pattern.

Drill 63. *Long Pass 4*

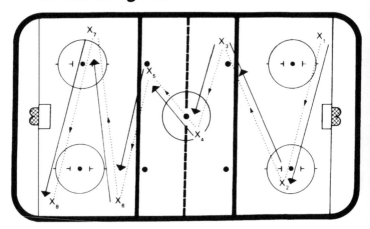

Purpose:
To provide a drill to teach long passes and player movement.

Description:
Players are lined up along the ice in a pattern which keeps long distances between opposite players. Player makes the pass to the next player and follows the puck to that player. For example, X_1 passes to X_2 and moves to where X_2 is. X_2 passes to X_3 and moves to X_3.

Tempo:
Drill is executed from 3/4 to full speed.

Participation:
The entire team. Team can be divided into groups of a few players (4-6).

Variation:
The number of players can change.

Drill 64. *"Move the Puck"*

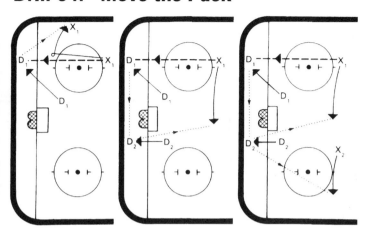

Purpose:
To provide a drill to teach defensemen to move the puck quickly in their own end and forward to position themselves to receive quick passes.

Description:
Two (2) players, a forward (X_1) and a defenseman (D_1), work this drill. X_1 dumps the puck in the corner, and D_1 moves to the corner. D_1 moves the puck quickly to X_1 who has moved to the boards.

Tempo:
Drill is executed at full speed.

Participation:
Drill can be practiced at both ends of the ice or only one end.

Variations:
Players can be added. For example, D_1 to X_1 or X_2; D_1 to X_1 back to D_1; D_1 to D_2 to X_1 or X_2.

Drill 65. *Drop Pass*

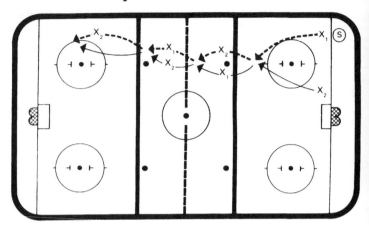

Purpose:
To provide a drill to teach the drop pass.

Description:
X_1 skates with the puck, X_2 comes from behind and X_1 drop passes to X_2. X_2 proceeds with the puck and X_1 slows down and then comes from behind for a drop pass from X_2. Drill is executed around the rink.

Tempo:
Drill is started at a slow speed and is increased as the passing skill is improved.

Participation:
The entire team, second pair starts after first pair clears the near blue line.

Drill 66. *Board Pass 1*

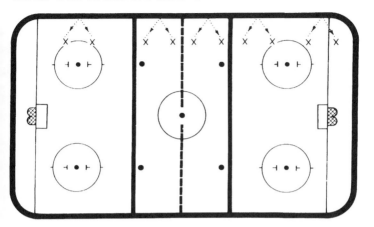

Purpose:
To provide a drill to teach the use of the boards while passing.

Description:
Players are spread around the ice and work in pairs. The players direct the passes to each other by banking the puck off the boards. Players should make passes both on the forehand and the backhand as well as receive the passes the same way.

Tempo:
Drill is started with slow easy passes and progresses to crisp quick passes.

Participation:
The entire team.

Variations:
The player makes short movements.

Drill 67. *Board Pass 2*

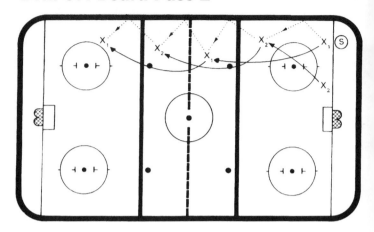

Purpose:
To provide a drill to teach the use of boards while passing to a moving player.

Description:
Players work in pairs and move around the ice in a lap like fashion. In this drill, one player is stationary and one is moving. X_1 is stationary and passes to X_2 who is moving with a board pass. X_1 then moves ahead of X_2 to take a board pass.

Tempo:
Drill is executed at a slow speed and is increased as the passing skill is improved.

Participation:
The entire team.

Drill 68. *Board Pass 3*

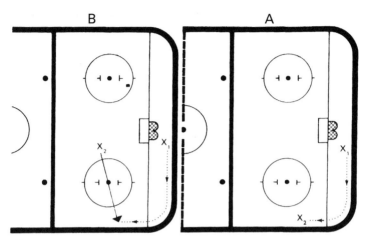

Purpose:
To provide a drill to teach the use of the board pass to clear the defensive zone.

Description:
In this drill, X_1 passes to X_2 who is on the boards (Diagram A). This drill teaches both the art of passing along the boards and of receiving a board pass. Drill should progress to point that X_2 can move to the boards and simultaneously receive the pass (Diagram B).

Tempo:
Drill is executed at a slow speed and is increased as the passing skill is improved.

Participation:
Drill can be executed in the four (4) corners.

Drill 69. *Back Pass 1*

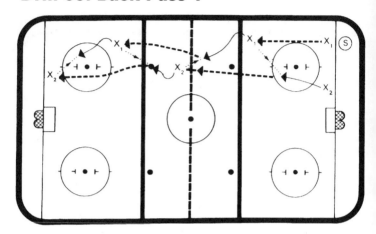

Purpose:
To provide a drill to teach the back pass.

Description:
Performed with two (2) players as a pair. X_1, with a
puck, moves ahead of X_2 and makes a backpass to X_2.
X_2 then moves ahead of X_1 and makes a backpass to X_1.

Tempo:
Drill is executed at a slow speed and is increased as the
passing skill is improved.

Participation:
The entire team.

Variations:
Have a third player join the pair and the three (3) work
the drill as a unit.

Drill 70. *Back Pass 2*

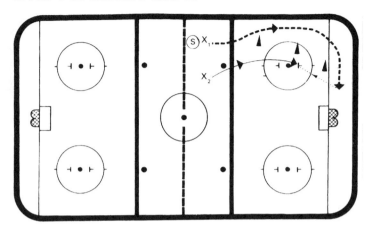

Purpose:

To provide a drill to teach the back pass in the slot area.

Description:

Performed with two (2) players moving toward the net along the boards. The first player, X_1, carries the puck deep behind the goal line. The second player, X_2, moves toward the slot area. X_1 makes a back pass to X_2 in the slot area.

Tempo:

Drill is executed from 3/4 to full speed.

Participation:

Team is divided into four (4) groups, two (2) in each end.

Drill 71. *Head Man Pass*

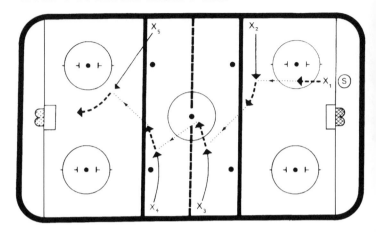

Purpose:

To provide a drill to teach quick puck advancement to the "head man".

Description:

Players are grouped (X_1 to X_5) at different spots on the ice. The puck is moved quickly to the next player who is skating ahead to force the pass. This is a quick tempo drill, and the head man must be moving to force the quick head pass. X_1 passes to X_2 and moves to X_2's spot, X_2 to X_3 and so on.

Tempo:

Drill is executed from 3/4 to full speed.

Participation:

The entire team. Team can be divided into groups (4-8).

Variations:

Change the number of groups to dictate long and short passes; groups align themselves at different places on the ice.

Drill 72. *Breakout Pass*

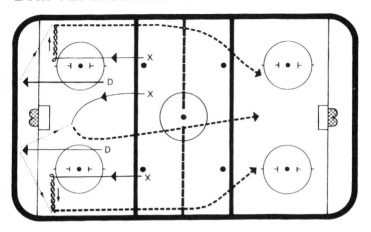

Purpose:
To provide a drill that simulates the passing patterns of the team's breakout system.

Description:
The players execute the positional passing patterns of the team's breakout system. Practice the players receiving the passes at different places in the patterns. The players should interchange with the different positions to be familiar with the different patterns.

Tempo:
Drill is executed from 3/4 to full speed.

Participation:
Team is divided into five (5) man units. Drill can also be executed with just the forwards or the defensemen.

Drill 73. *Offensive Zone Passing*

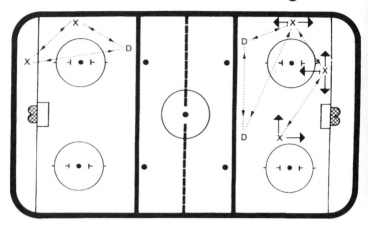

Purpose:
To provide a drill to teach the passing patterns in the offensive zone.

Description:
The players pass the puck around in the offensive zone. This drill enables work to be made for specific situations. Drill teaches the offensive unit anticipation with each other and movement as a total unit.

Tempo:
Drill is executed at full speed.

Participation:
Team is divided into five (5) man units and can be executed at both ends.

Variations:
Fewer players can be used to work on specific plays.

Drill 74. *Passing Game*

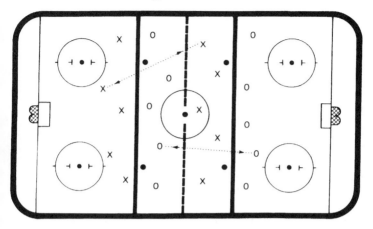

Purpose:
To provide a drill for competition to utilize the passing skills.

Description:
Two (2) teams, X's and O's. Teams are aligned as in the diagram. The X's attempt to keep the puck while passing between the two (2) groups of X's. The O's attempt to gain control of the puck and keep it from the X's.

Tempo:
Players will dictate the tempo, usually full speed.

Participation:
The entire team, divided into two (2) teams.

Variations:
Add additional pucks but not too many. Three (3) is usually the limit.

Drill 75. *Relay Races*

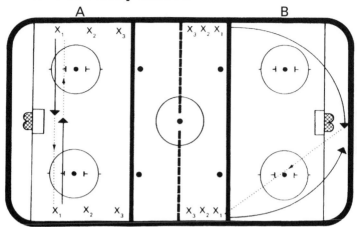

Purpose:

To provide a drill that is competitive to utilize the passing skills.

Description:

Team is divided into groups and competitive passing games are played: (A) Players skate to the middle and pass to a group member on the opposite board; (B) Players skate behind the net and pass to a group member at the red line.

Tempo:

Drill is executed at full speed.

Participation:

The entire team. Team is divided into groups. Normally, the groups should have 4-8 players.

CHAPTER 4

Shooting

"Home is the sailor, home from sea,
   And the hunter, home from the hill."

Robert Louis Stevenson
Requiem

Drill 76. *Stationary Shooting*

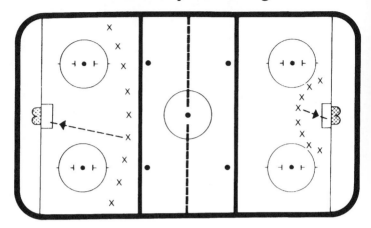

Purpose:
To provide a warm-up shooting drill.

Description:
Performed with the players stationary and shooting from that position. Distances can be varied, i.e., from the blue line, half-way between the net and blue line, close to the net. Practice the different shots: wrist, snap, backhand, and slap.

Tempo:
Drill is executed from 3/4 to full speed.

Participation:
The entire team, half at each end.

Variations:
Players take a couple strides before shooting; players take a pass from the corner before shooting; players shoot 2-3 pucks at a time.

Drill 77. *Swing-out*

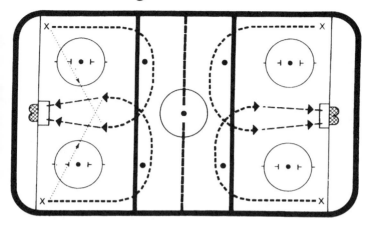

Purpose:

To provide a warm-up shooting drill while skating.

Description:

Performed with players rotating out of the corners. Players skate from corner past the blue line and swing in toward the net. Practice the different shots and vary the distances.

Tempo:

Drill is executed from 3/4 to full speed.

Participation:

The entire team, half at each end.

Variations:

Many options can be used, i.e., pass from opposite corner to swinging shooter; pass behind the net around the boards to shooter who takes pass and then swings out; alternating forward and backward skating (skate backwards, take pass, turn and skate forward to shoot) are some examples.

Drill 78. *Break-off the Wings 1*

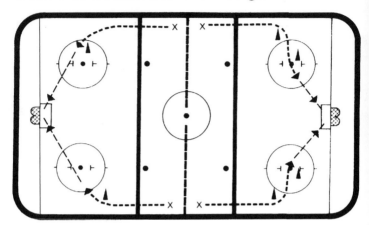

Purpose:

To provide a drill that has the players breaking off the wings to shoot.

Description:

Performed with players skating down the boards and shooting coming off the boards. Obstacles can be placed to set patterns the shooters will follow. Practice the different shots and vary the distances.

Tempo:

Drill is executed from 3/4 to full speed.

Participation:

The entire team, half at each end. Drill starts near the red line on the boards.

Variations:

Players can take passes to start drill; change the patterns by moving the obstacles.

Drill 79. *Break-off the Wings 2*

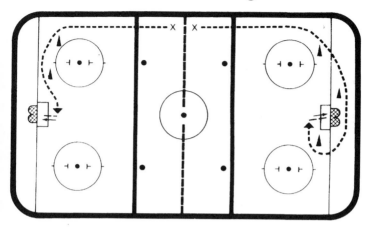

Purpose:
To provide a drill that has the players breaking off the wings to shoot.

Description:
Performed with players skating down the boards and carrying the puck deep. Obstacles are placed to set the pattern for the shooter to go for the net. The patterns can vary.

Tempo:
Drill is executed from 3/4 to full speed.

Participation:
The entire team, half at each end. Drill starts near the red line on the boards.

Variations:
Players can take passes to start the drill; change the patterns by moving the obstacles.

Drill 80. *Break-off the Wings 3*

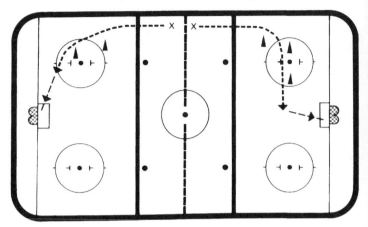

Purpose:
To provide a drill that has the players breaking off the wings to shoot.

Description:
Performed with players skating down the boards and shooting coming off the boards. Obstacles are placed to set the pattern for the shooter. Both forehand and backhand shots should be practiced.

Tempo:
Drill is executed from 3/4 to full speed.

Participation:
The entire team, half at each end. Drill starts near the red line on the boards.

Variations:
Players can take passes to start the drill; change the patterns by moving the obstacles.

Drill 81. *Pass and Shoot 1*

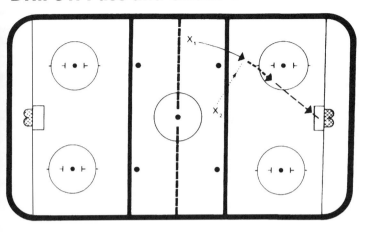

Purpose:
To provide a drill to combine passing and shooting.

Description:
Performed with a player (X_1) breaking off the boards, taking a pass from a second player (X_2), and shooting the puck.

Tempo:
Drill is executed from 3/4 to full speed.

Participation:
The entire team, half at each end. Drill starts near the red line on the boards.

Variations:
Player passing the puck moves around to change the spot from where he passes.

Drill 82. *Pass and Shoot 2*

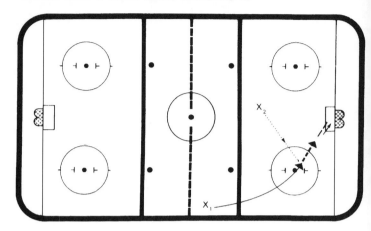

Purpose:

To provide a drill to combine passing and shooting.

Description:

Performed with a player (X_1) breaking to the net from the blue line, taking a pass from a second player (X_2) who is in the middle of the ice, and shooting the puck.

Tempo:

Drill is executed from 3/4 to full speed.

Participation:

The entire team, half at each end. Drill starts near the red line on the boards.

Variations:

Player passing the puck moves around to change the spot from where he passes.

Drill 83. *Pass and Shoot 3*

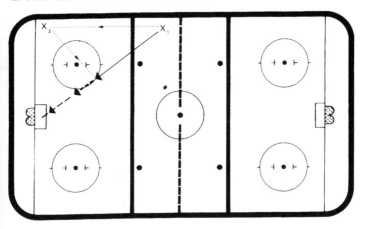

Purpose:
To provide a drill to combine passing and shooting.

Description:
Performed with a player (X_1) breaking-off the boards and a second player (X_2) in the corner passing the puck. X_1 initiates drill by passing to X_2 and breaking for the net for a return pass.

Tempo:
Drill is executed from 3/4 to full speed.

Participation:
The entire team, half at each end. Drill starts near the red line on the boards.

Variations:
Player passing the puck moves around to change the spot from where he passes.

Drill 84. *Pass and Shoot 4*

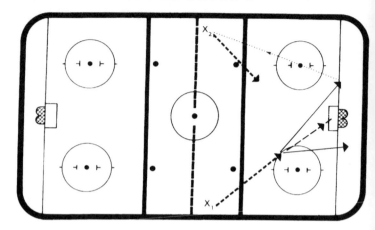

Purpose:
To provide a drill to combine passing and shooting.

Description:
Performed with players on both sides of the ice at the red line. The first player (X_1) skates in and shoots. He then picks up his own rebound (if he scores, there are loose pucks in the corner) and passes to the second player (X_2). The second player does the same.

Tempo:
Drill is executed at full speed.

Participation:
The entire team, half at each end.

Drill 85. *Pass and Shoot 5*

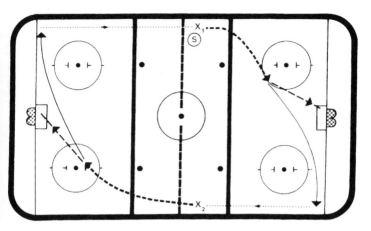

Purpose:

To provide a drill to combine passing and shooting.

Description:

Drill utilizes the whole ice surface with team divided into two (2) groups. The groups are opposite each other at the red line. Loose pucks are in the corners opposite to the players. The first player (X_1) carries the puck and shoots. He proceeds to the corner, picks up a loose puck and passes to a player in the other group (X_2). The second player (X_2) does the same.

Tempo:

Drill is executed at full speed.

Participation:

The entire team.

Variations:

Players can be placed at different spots to be involved in the passing but not the shooting.

Drill 86. *Pass and Shoot 6*

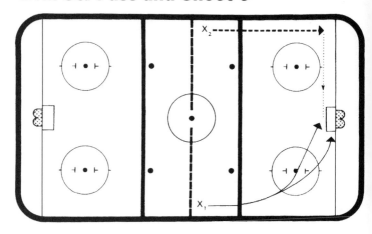

Purpose:

To provide a drill to combine passing and shooting.

Description:

Performed with players on both sides of the ice at the red line. The first player (X_2) carries the puck deep into the end. The second player (X_1) skates into the zone and to the slot area. X_2 passes the puck to X_1 who is breaking to the net for the shot.

Tempo:

Drill is executed at full speed.

Participation:

The entire team, half at each end.

Variations:

Obstacles can be added to make the drill more difficult.

Drill 87. *Rebound Shots*

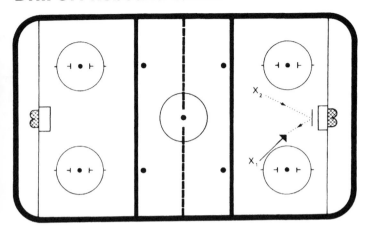

Purpose:

To provide a drill to practice getting rebounds.

Description:

A bench is laid across the goalmouth. One player (X_2) shoots puck against the bench. The second player (X_1) breaks for the net, goes for the rebound, and must get his shot over the bench.

Tempo:

Drill is executed at full speed.

Participation:

The entire team, half at each end.

Drill 88. *Backhand Shots*

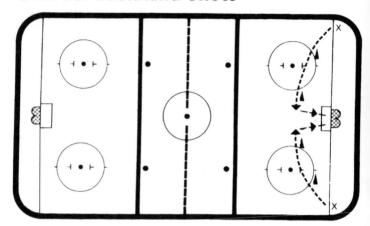

Purpose:

To provide a drill to practice backhand shots.

Description:

Performed with players skating out of the corners to the net. Obstacles can be placed to set patterns. Practice the backhand shots.

Tempo:

Drill is executed at full speed.

Participation:

The entire team. Left hand shooters are in one corner and right hand shooters in the other corner.

Drill 89. *Pass and Shoot 7*

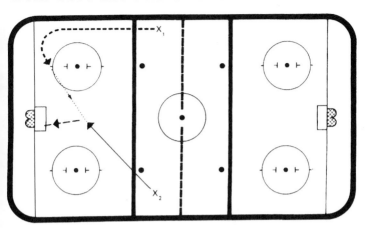

Purpose:

To provide a drill to combine passing and shooting.

Description:

Performed with players on both sides of the ice. The first player (X_1) carries the puck deep into the corner. The second player (X_2) skates into the zone to the slot area. X_1 passes the puck to X_2 who is breaking into the slot for the shot.

Tempo:

Drill is executed at full speed.

Participation:

The entire team, half at each end.

Variations:

Obstacles can be added to make the drill more difficult.

Drill 90. *Tip-ins 1*

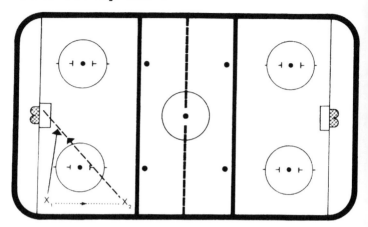

Purpose:
To provide a drill to practice tip-in shots.

Description:
Performed with a player (X_1) in the corner and a player (X_2) on the blue line. X_1 begins the drill by passing to X_2. X_1 moves to the front of the net to position himself to tip-in the shot from X_2.

Tempo:
Drill is executed at full speed.

Participation:
The entire team. Drill can be worked out of four (4) corners.

Variations:
Obstacles can be inserted to force X_1 to work to gain position.

Drill 91. *Tip-ins 2*

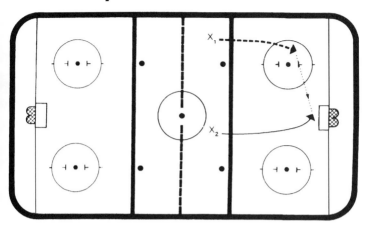

Purpose:
To provide a drill to practice tip-in shots.

Description:
Performed with two players. The first player (X_1) carries the puck deep along the boards. The second player (X_2) breaks for the net. X_1 passes the puck toward the net, across the goalmouth, and X_2 deflects or tip-ins the puck.

Tempo:
Drill is executed at full speed.

Participation:
The entire team, half at each end.

Variations:
Obstacles can be inserted in the slot area to make it more difficult to complete the pass/shot for the tip-in.

Drill 92. *Pass and Shoot 8*

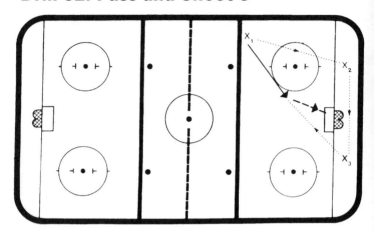

Purpose:
To provide a drill with passing, shooting and player movement.

Description:
Performed with three (3) players. X_1 passes to X_2 and moves into the slot. X_2 passes to X_3 who passes to X_1 in the slot for the shot. X_1 moves to X_3's spot, X_3 to X_2's and X_2 to X_1's.

Tempo:
Drill is executed at full speed.

Participation:
The entire team, half at each end.

Variations:
The three (3) players can change where they are located on the ice.

Drill 93. *Pass and Shoot 9*

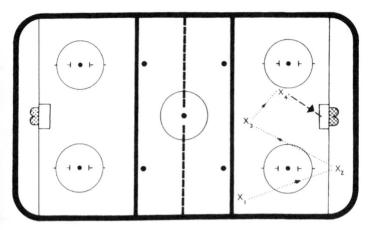

Purpose:

To provide a drill with passing, shooting, and player movement.

Description:

Performed with four (4) players. X_1 passes to X_2, X_2 passes to X_3, X_3 passes to X_4 in the slot for the shot. X_1 moves to X_2's spot, X_2 to X_3's, X_3 to X_4's, and X_4 to X_1's.

Tempo:

Drill is executed at full speed.

Participation:

The entire team, half at each end.

Variations:

The four (4) players can change where they are located on the ice.

Drill 94. *Pass and Shoot 10*

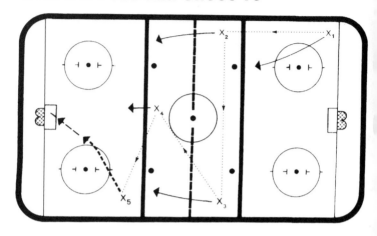

Purpose:
To provide a drill with passing, shooting, and player movement.

Description:
Performed with five (5) players. X_1 passes to X_2, X_2 passes to X_3, X_3 passes to X_4, and X_4 passes to X_5. Each player moves into the play so that when X_5 gets the puck, there are five (5) players moving toward the net as a unit.

Tempo:
Drill is executed at full speed.

Participation:
The entire team. Team is divided into five (5) man units.

Variations:
Obstacles can be inserted to make drill more difficult.

Drill 95. *Pass and Shoot 11*

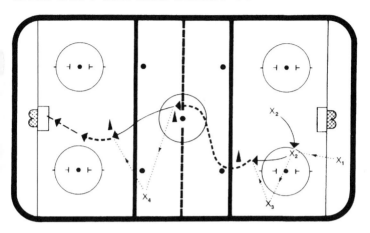

Purpose:

To provide a drill with passing, shooting, and player movement.

Description:

Performed with four (4) players. X_1 passes to X_2, X_2 passes to X_3 and moves up the ice for return pass. X_2 passes to X_4 and continues to move up the ice for return pass and takes shot. X_1 moves to X_2's spot, X_2 to X_4's, X_3 to X_1's, and X_4 to X_3's.

Tempo:

Drill is executed at full speed.

Participation:

The entire team.

Variations:

Change the patterns with the obstacles.

Drill 96. *Multiple Shots 1*

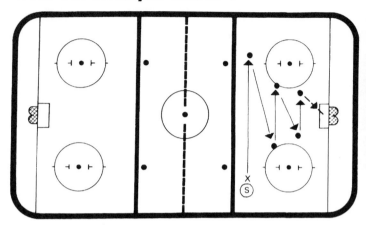

Purpose:
To provide a drill for players to take a number of shots from different spots on the ice.

Description:
Pucks are placed in a pattern that has the shooter skate back and forth. Each puck is closer to the net. The shooter skates to each puck for the shots. He takes both forehand and backhand shots. Use 4-10 pucks.

Tempo:
Drill is executed at full speed.

Participation:
The entire team, half at each end.

Variations:
Change the patterns of the pucks.

Drill 97. *Multiple Shots 2*

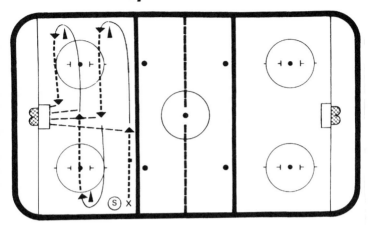

Purpose:

To provide a drill for players to take a number of shots from different spots on the ice.

Description:

Pucks are placed along the boards with each one deeper in the zone. The player picks up the first puck, skates to the middle, shoots, continues to the other side, picks up a puck, skates to the middle and shoots. Obstacles are placed on the boards for the shooter to swing around. Use 4-10 pucks.

Tempo:

Drill is executed at full speed.

Participation:

The entire team, half at each end.

Variations:

Change the location of the obstacles.

Drill 98. *Multiple Shots 3*

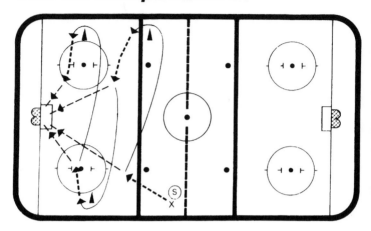

Purpose:

To provide a drill for players to take a number of shots from different spots on the ice.

Description:

Pucks are placed along the boards and 10-15 feet in from the boards. The player picks up the first puck, skates toward the net and shoots, continues to the other side, picks up a puck, skates toward the net and shoots. Obstacles are placed to have the player skate around. Use 4-10 pucks.

Tempo:

Drill is executed at full speed.

Participation:

The entire team, half at each end.

Variations:

Change the location of the obstacles.

Drill 99. *Multiple Shots* 4

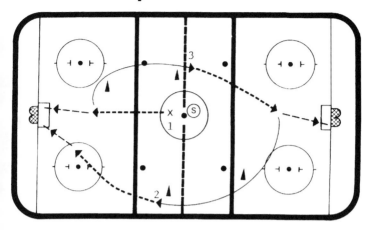

Purpose:
To provide a drill for players to take a number of shots from different spots on the ice.

Description:
Pucks are placed in three (3) spots in the neutral zone. The player starts at one spot, skates in and shoots. He then swings back to the neutral zone, picks up a second puck, skates in and shoots. He does the same for the third puck. Obstacles are placed for the player to skate around.

Tempo:
Drill is executed at full speed.

Participation:
The entire team, one player at a time. This is a good competitive type game drill. Players keep track of goals. Play till there is a winner.

Variations:
Change the location of the pucks.

Drill 100. *First To Score*

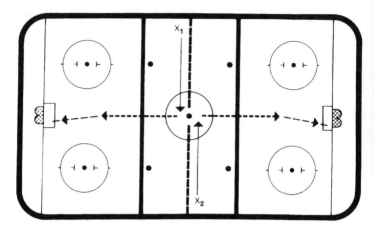

Purpose:

To provide a competitive shooting drill.

Description:

Performed with two (2) players. Players line up on red line on opposite boards. On the whistle, they skate to center ice and each picks up a puck. The first to score is the winner. Normally, the winners continue to play against other winners until there is a final winner.

Tempo:

Drill is executed at full speed.

Participation:

The entire team.

Variations:

Increase the number of pucks, three (3) should be the maximum.

CHAPTER 5

Conditioning

Drill 101. *Intervals 1*

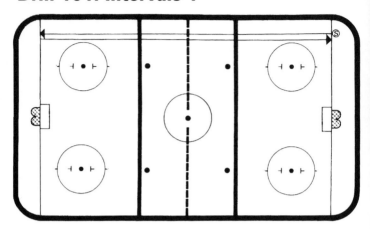

Purpose:
To provide a drill for anaerobic conditioning.

Description:
Performed by skating from goal line to goal line, stop, and back.

Participation:
Team is divided into three (3) to five (5) groups.

Intervals:
1:3 to 1:5. 8 to 12 repetitions. 80 to 85% intensity.

Note:
1:3 means work one (1) interval, rest three (3) intervals;

1:5 means work one (1) interval, rest five (5) intervals.

Drill 102. *Intervals 2*

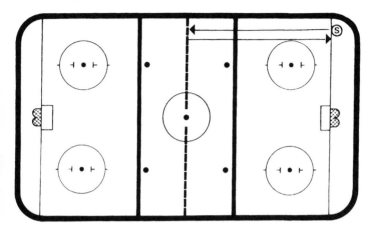

Purpose:
To provide a drill for anaerobic conditioning.

Description:
Performed by skating from goal line to red line, stop, and back.

Participation:
Team is divided into three (3) to five (5) groups.

Intervals:
1:3 to 1:5. 8 to 12 repetitions. 90 to 100% intensity.

Drill 103. *Intervals 3*

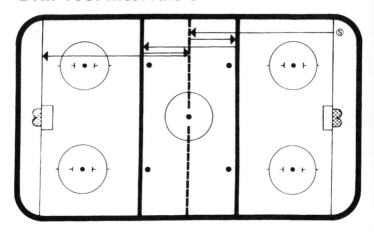

Purpose:
To provide a drill for anaerobic conditioning.

Description:
Performed by skating from goal line to red line, stop, to near blue line, stop, to far blue line, stop, to red line, stop, to far goal line.

Participation:
Team is divided into three (3) to five (5) groups.

Intervals:
1:3 to 1:5. 8 to 12 repetitions. 80 to 85% intensity.

Drill 104. *Intervals 4*

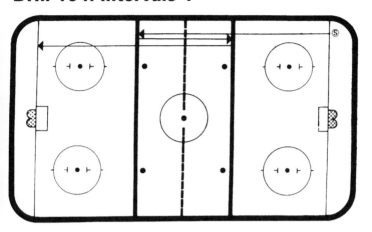

Purpose:
To provide a drill for anaerobic conditioning.

Description:
Performed by skating from goal line to far blue line,
stop, to near blue line, stop, to far goal line.

Participation:
Team is divided into three (3) to five (5) groups.

Intervals:
1:3 to 1:5. 8 to 12 repetitions. 80 to 85% intensity.

Drill 105. *Time Intervals 1*

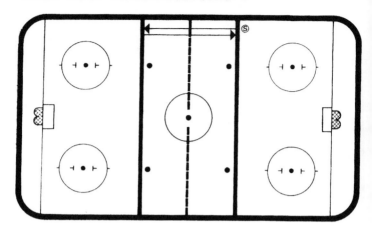

Purpose:
To provide a drill for anaerobic conditioning.

Description:
Performed by skating from blue line to blue line, stop, back to blue line. Drill is executed for a specific time period.

Participation:
Team is divided into two (2) to four (4) groups.

Intervals:
1:3 to 1:4. (If team is divided into two (2) groups, during one or two intervals, neither group would be skating). 4 to 8 repetitions. 80 to 90% intensity. Time Period: 15 to 30 seconds.

Drill 106. *Time Intervals 2*

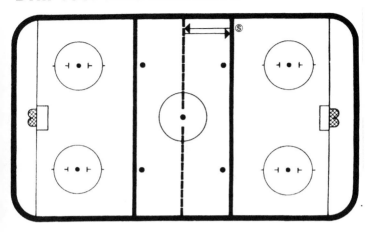

Purpose:
To provide a drill for anaerobic conditioning.

Description:
Performed by skating from blue line to red line, stop, back to blue line. Drill is executed for a specific time period.

Participation:
Team is divided into two (2) to four (4) groups.

Intervals:
1:3 to 1:4. (If a team is divided into two (2) groups, during one or two intervals, neither group would be skating). 4 to 8 repetitions. 80 to 90% intensity. Time Period: 15 to 30 seconds.

Drill 107. *Laps 1*

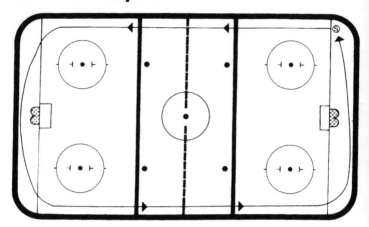

Purpose:
To provide a drill for anaerobic conditioning.

Description:
Performed by skating a full lap.

Participation:
Team is divided into three (3) to five (5) groups.

Intervals:
1:3 to 1:5. 8 to 12 repetitions. 80 to 85% intensity.

Drill 108. *Laps 2*

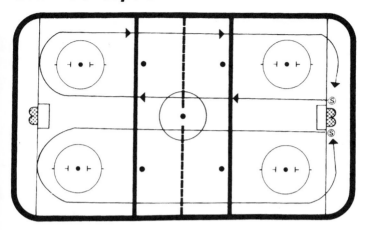

Purpose:

To provide a drill for anaerobic conditioning.

Description:

Performed by skating up the middle, swing deep into the corners, and back along the boards.

Participation:

Team is divided into three (3) to five (5) groups.

Intervals:

1:3 to 1:5. 8 to 12 repetitions. 80 to 85% intensity.

Drill 109. *Laps 3*

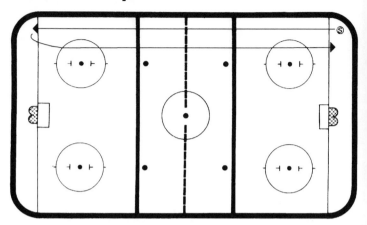

Purpose:

To provide a drill for anaerobic conditioning.

Description:

Players skate the length of the ice, turn, and come back easy.

Participation:

Team is divided into three (3) to five (5) groups.

Intervals:

1:3 to 1:5. 8 to 12 repetitions. 90 to 100% intensity.

Drill 110. *Laps 4*

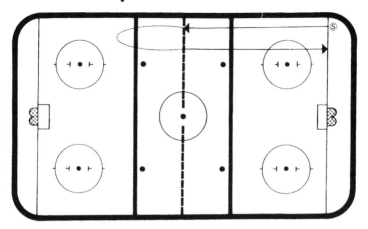

Purpose:
To provide a drill for anaerobic conditioning.

Description:
Performed by skating to red line, swing toward far blue line, and come back hard from red line to goal line.

Participation:
Team is divided into three (3) to five (5) groups.

Intervals:
1:3 to 1:5. 8 to 12 repetitions. 90 to 100% intensity.

Drill 111. *Intervals 5*

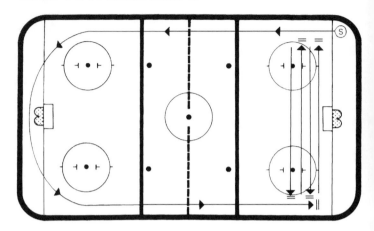

Purpose:

To provide a drill for anaerobic conditioning.

Description:

Performed by skating a lap (from goal line, around the opposite goal, and back to the goal line), then back and forth across the ice twice.

Participation:

Team is divided into four (4) to six (6) groups. There should be only three (3) to five (5) players in each group.

Intervals:

1:4 to 1:6. 6 to 8 repetitions. 70 to 80% intensity.

Drill 112. *Intervals 6*

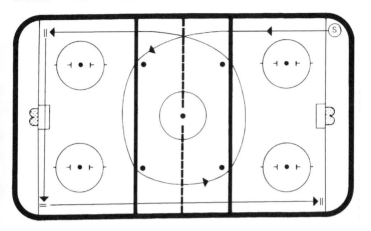

Purpose:

To provide a drill for anaerobic conditioning.

Description:

Performed by making a big loop in the neutral zone
ending up at the opposite end of the ice, skate across the
ice and stop, and skate the length of the ice and stop.

Participation:

Team is divided into four (4) to six (6) groups. There
should be only three (3) to five (5) players in each group.

Intervals:

1:4 to 1:6. 6 to 8 repetitions. 70 to 80% intensity.

Drill 113. *Intervals 7*

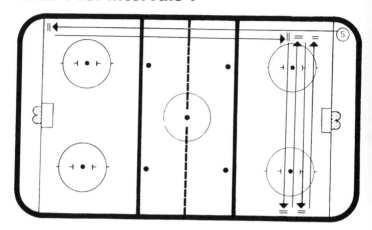

Purpose:
To provide a drill for anaerobic conditioning.

Description:
Performed by skating the length of the ice, stop, and back, then back and forth across the ice twice.

Participation:
Team is divided into four (4) to six (6) groups. There should only be three (3) to five (5) players in each group.

Intervals:
1:4 to 1:6. 6 to 8 repetitions. 70 to 80% intensity.

Drill 114. *"Let's Dance"*

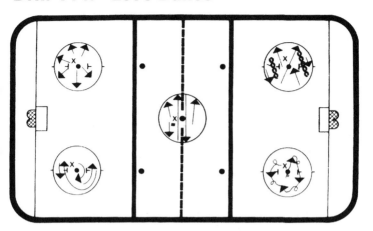

Purpose:
To provide a drill for anaerobic conditioning.

Description:
Performed with one (1) player in each face-off circle.
The players, for a specific time period, make constant
movement. Movement can be any type of activity:
skating, exercises, dance moves, etc.

Participation:
Team is divided into five (5) man units.

Intervals:
1:3 to 1:4. 4 to 6 repetitions. 90 to 100% intensity. Time
Period: 15-30 seconds.

Drill 115. *Laps 5*

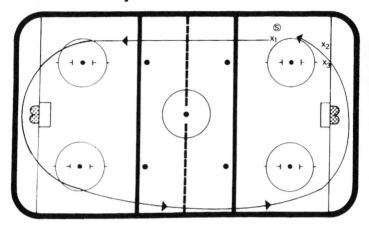

Purpose:

To provide a drill for anaerobic conditioning.

Description:

Performed with one (1) player on top of the face-off circle and two (2) to four (4) on the goal line. The group of players chase X_1. An option is to have a different player take the lead for each lap and to keep the times between groups.

Participation:

The entire team.

Intervals:

1:4 to 1:6. 80 to 85% intensity. Time Period: 15 to 60 seconds.

Drill 116. *Intervals 8*

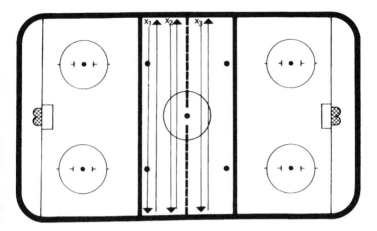

Purpose:
To provide a drill for anaerobic conditioning.

Description:
Players skate across the ice, stop, and come back.
Performed in groups of three (3), first player goes,
followed by second and then third players.

Participation:
The entire team, team is divided into groups of three.

Intervals:
1:2. 8 to 12 repetitions. 80 to 90% intensity.

Drill 117. *Intervals 9*

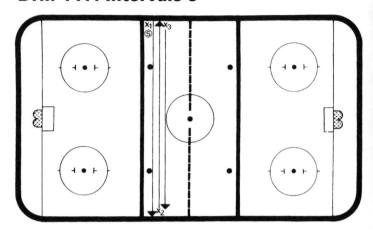

Purpose:

To provide a drill for anaerobic conditioning.

Description:

Performed in groups of three (3). One (1) player is on one side and the other two (2) are on the opposite side. Drill consists of players skating across the ice. X_1 starts drill by skating across the ice and stops. X_2 does the same as does X_3. The players simply rotate.

Participation:

The entire team.

Intervals:

1:2. 8 to 12 repetitions. 100% intensity.

Drill 118. *Retrieves Pucks*

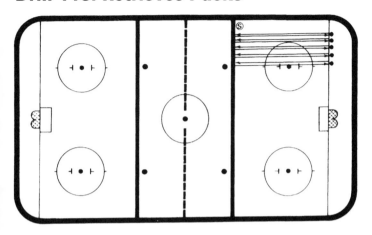

Purpose:

To provide a drill for anaerobic conditioning.

Description:

Pucks (3-5) are lined up on the blue line. A player skates
from the goal line to the blue line, stops, picks up a
puck, skates back to goal line, stops, drops the puck,
continues on for the other pucks.

Participation:

The entire team. Players can work in groups of two (2)
or four (4). First player brings pucks back to goal line,
second player takes pucks to the blue line, and so forth.

Intervals:

1:4. 80 to 90% intensity.

Drill 119. *2-0/1-1*

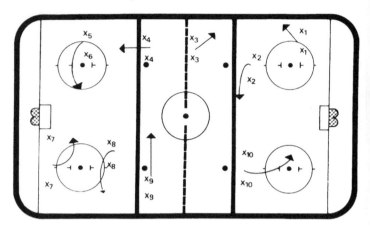

Purpose:
To provide a competitive drill for anaerobic conditioning.

Description:
Performed in pairs. Drill is divided into three (3) segments: 2-0, 1-1, rest. 2-0 segment has players passing the puck back and forth. 1-1 segment has two players fighting for control of the puck. Rest segment is light skating.

Participation:
The entire team.

Intervals:
1:1:2 (2-0, 1-1, rest). 4 to 8 repetitions. 85 to 90% intensity. Time Intervals: 10 to 15 seconds.

Drill 120. *Breakout*

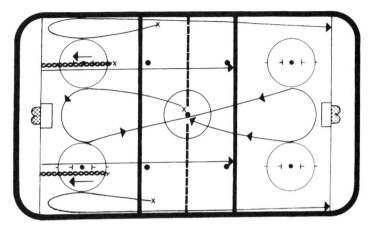

Purpose:

To provide a drill for anaerobic conditioning with the team's breakout system.

Description:

The players execute the positional breakout patterns for coming out of their own end. The players should interchange with the different positions to be familiar with the different patterns.

Participation:

Team is divided into five (5) man units.

Intervals:

1:3 or 1:4. For short anaerobic bursts at 95 to 100%, each unit would go right after each other. For longer anaerobic training, time periods of 20 to 40 seconds can be used. This means that the units would make multiple rushes and can do it both ways or go one way, return, and go again.

Drill 121. *Aerobic 1*

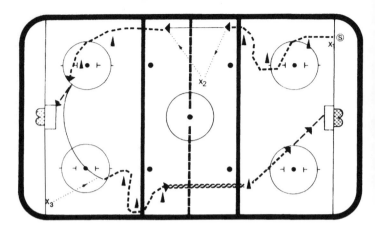

Purpose:

To provide a drill for aerobic conditioning.

Description:

Performed by combining different skill drills while skating a lap. X_1 starts by skating through the obstacles with a puck, then passes to X_2 and receives a return pass and continues on for a shot. X_1 then swings across the ice and receives a pass from X_3, moves up the ice with the puck, turns at the red line and skates backwards to the blue line, turns, and goes in for a shot.

Participation:

Team is divided into two (2) groups, one (1) is on the ice, the other rests. Groups execute the drill for a specific time period with continuous activity. Players repeat drill several times during the time period.

Intervals:

60 to 80% intensity. Time Period: 5 to 8 minutes.

Drill 122. *Aerobic 2*

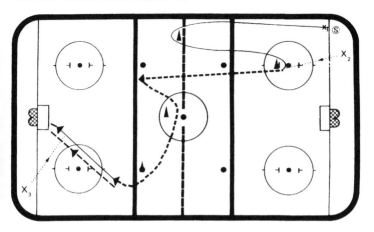

Purpose:

To provide a drill for aerobic conditioning.

Description:

Performed by combining different skill drills. X_1 starts by skating to the red line, swinging around the obstacle and back around the obstacle in the face-off circle. He receives a pass from X_2, and skates up the ice following the pattern laid out with obstacles. X_1 takes a long shot from the blue line, breaks for the net, receives a pass from X_3 and takes a second shot. X_1 then returns to the starting point.

Participation:

Team is divided into two (2) groups, one (1) is on the ice, the other rests. Groups execute the drill for a specific time period with continuous activity. Players repeat drill several times during the time period.

Intervals:

60 to 80% intensity. Time Period: 5 to 8 minutes.

Drill 123. *Aerobic 3*

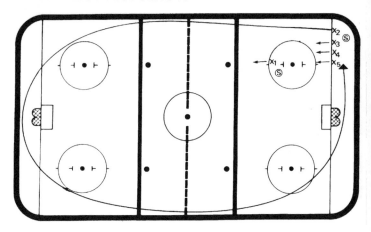

Purpose:

To provide a drill for aerobic conditioning.

Description:

Players skate laps for a specific time period. Each group of players skate as a group and stay together. Each player should take turns leading the group.

Participation:

Team is divided into groups of 4 to 6 players. Two (2) groups execute the drill simultaneously while the others rest.

Intervals:

60 to 80% intensity. Time Period: 5 to 8 minutes.

Drill 124. *Winner Rests*

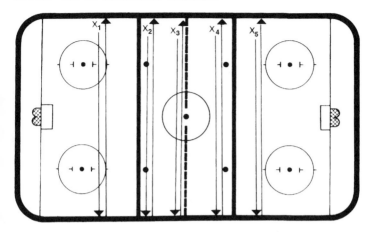

Purpose:

To provide a competitive conditioning drill.

Description:

Performed with players lined up along the boards.
Players skate to far boards, stop, and return. Winner gets to rest.

Participation:

The entire team.

Tempo:

Drill is executed at full speed.

Variations:

Drill can be executed with laps, or over and back twice, or red line to blue line and back, etc.

Drill 125. *1 on 1 Conditioning*

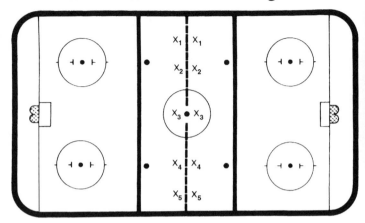

Purpose:

To provide a conditioning drill that is competitive.

Description:

Games of 1 on 1 are played simultaneously. Drill is executed for specific time period.

Participation:

The entire team. Part or all the players can execute the drill. Players can use the entire ice or be limited (i.e., 1 on 1 games in each zone).

Intervals:

90 to 100% intensity. Time Period: 30 to 120 seconds.

CHAPTER 6

Goaltending

"But once again, my belief was substantiated that a youngster must practice self-discipline and get his game under control if he is to reach individual stardom and the team success."

John Wooden
They Call Me Coach

Drill 126. *Warm-up*

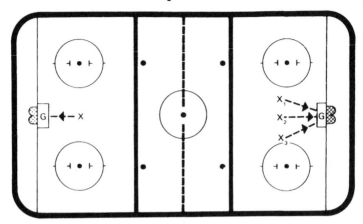

Purpose:

To provide a warm-up drill for goalies.

Description:

Performed with one (1) or three (3) players taking shots at the goalie. Shots are easy, directed at specific spots (i.e., catching glove, blocker, lower left side, etc.). Drill enables goalie to loosen up and get the feel of the puck.

Participation:

Goalie, small number of shooters.

Drill 127. *Random Shots 1*

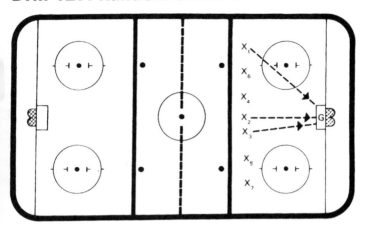

Purpose:

To provide a warm-up drill for goalies.

Description:

Performed with a number (5-12) players lined up across the ice in front of the goalie. The distance can vary. Each player has a number, unknown to the goalie. The orders of shooting follows the numbers of the players. This forces the goalie to react quickly to the person shooting.

Participation:

Goalie, large number of shooters.

Drill 128. *Random Shots 2*

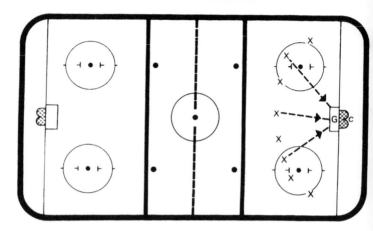

Purpose:

To provide a warm-up drill for goalies.

Description:

Performed with a number (5-12) players lined up across the ice in front of the goalie. The distance can vary. The coach is behind the net. He points to the player that will shoot. This forces the goalie to react quickly to the person shooting. It also means the shooters are all prepared to shoot since they do not know who actually will be shooting.

Participation:

Goalie, large number of shooters, coach.

Drill 129. *Movement 1*

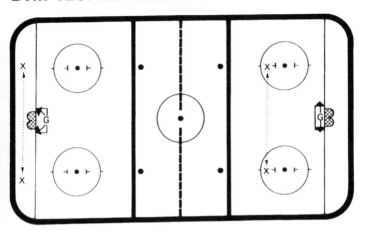

Purpose:
To provide a drill to train the goalie to move in his goal area.

Description:
Performed with two (2) players passing the puck between themselves. The goalie moves with the puck. If the players are in front, the goalie's movements are out high to cut down the angle of the potential shooter. If the players are behind the net, the goalie's movements are deep in the net to protect both goal posts.

Participation:
Goalie, two (2) players.

Drill 130. *Movement 2*

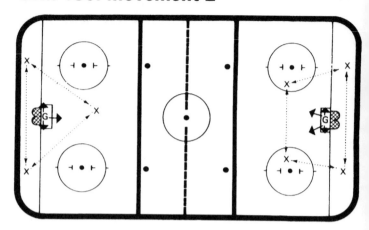

Purpose:

To provide a drill to train the goalie to move in his goal area.

Description:

Performed with three (3) or four (4) players passing the puck. The goalie moves with the puck. The three (3) players are in a triangle shape, and the four (4) players are in a box shape. The goalie has to move both in tight to protect the goal posts and out high to cut down the angle of potential shots.

Participation:

Goalie, three (3) or four (4) players.

Drill 131. *Movement 3*

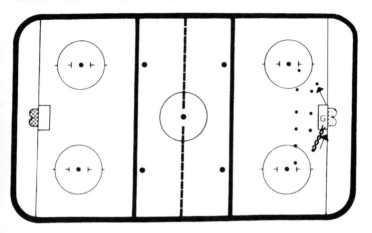

Purpose:

To provide a drill to train the goalie to move out and clear the puck.

Description:

Pucks are lined up 5 to 15 feet from the crease. The goalie moves out and clears the first puck, backs into his crease, moves out to clear the second puck, and so on. Practice clearing the puck both on forehand and backhand. Practice one-handed and two-handed clearing.

Participation:

Goalie.

Drill 132. *Movement 4*

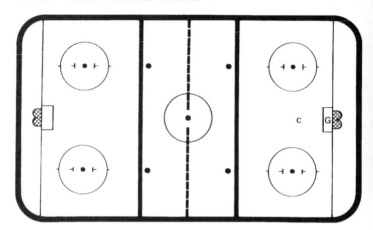

Purpose:

To provide a drill to train the goalie to make quick body movements.

Description:

The coach stands a few feet (7-10) in front of the goalie. The coach points with his stick in different directions and the goalie responds with the appropriate movement to make a save. The goalie, after each movement, returns quickly to his goalie stance. For example, the coach points high, the goalie moves to make a glove save. If he points low to the side, the goalie moves to make a leg save.

Participation:

Goalie, coach.

Drill 133. *Movement 5*

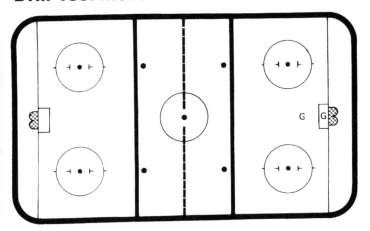

Purpose:
To provide a drill to train the goalie to make quick body movements.

Description:
Two (2) goalies stand five (5) feet apart. One goalie leads, the other follows. The lead goalie will make movements and the second goalie will follow. This "mirror" like drill teaches quick reactions.

Participation:
Two (2) goalies.

Drill 134. *Movement 6*

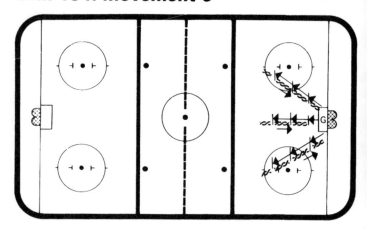

Purpose:

To provide a drill to train the goalie's agility.

Description:

Hockey sticks are laid down in front of the goal in some order, usually straight lines. The goalie, moving and maintaining his goalie stance, moves out stepping over the sticks. When he reaches the end, he moves backwards stepping over the sticks. A variation is to flip pucks high while goalie is moving for him to make glove saves.

Participation:

Goalie. A shooter.

Drill 135. *Movement 7*

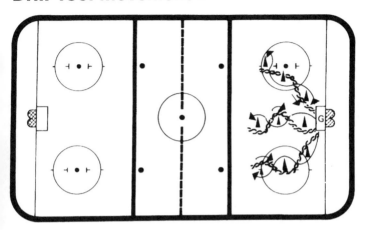

Purpose:

To provide a drill to train the goalie's agility.

Description:

Obstacles are laid out in front of the goal in some order, usually straight lines. The goalie, moving and maintaining his goalie stance, skates through the obstacles. When he reaches the end, he skates backwards to the goal. The goalie can also do the drill carrying a puck with his stick. Another variation is to flip pucks high while moving for the goalie to make glove saves.

Participation:

Goalie. A shooter.

Drill 136. *Movement 8*

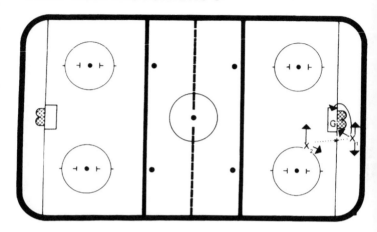

Purpose:
To provide a drill to train the goalie to make quick body movements.

Description:
Two (2) players, one in front and one behind the net, pass the puck back and forth. They also are moving in different directions. The goalie moves with the puck and with the players' movements. A variation is to give the players the option to shoot.

Participation:
Goalie, two (2) players.

Drill 137. *Shots 1*

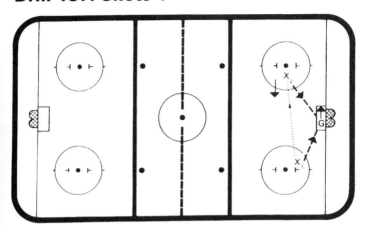

Purpose:

To provide a drill for goalies to stop shots after a pass.

Description:

Two players (X_1 and X_2) line up in front of the goal. X_1 can shoot or pass, X_2 can only shoot. The goalie must move with the pass.

Participation:

Goalie, two (2) players.

Drill 138. *Shots 2*

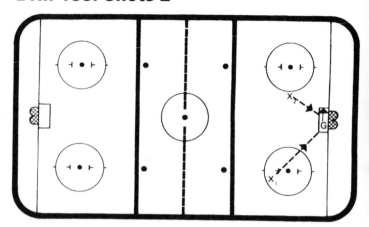

Purpose:

To provide a drill for goalies to stop shots and rebounds.

Description:

Two (2) players are in front of the goal. X_1 is 20 to 35 feet out, X_2 is 5 to 10 feet out. Both players have pucks. X_1 shoots. X_2 quickly shoots after X_1. Drill has X_1's shots from out and X_2's shots simulate rebounds. The goalie has to move quickly after making the first save.

Participation:

Goalie, two (2) players.

Drill 139. *Shots 3*

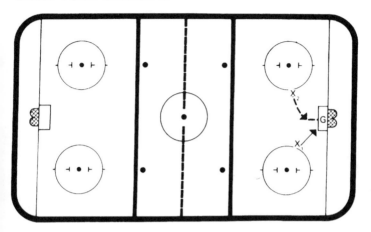

Purpose:
To provide a drill for goalies to stop shots and rebounds.

Description:
Two (2) players are in front of the goal. X_2 shoots and X_1 moves for rebound. Drill places emphasis on rebounds so X_2's shots are such that rebounds will usually result.

Participation:
Goalie, two (2) players.

Drill 140. *Shots 4*

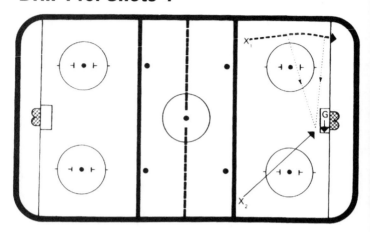

Purpose:

To provide a drill for goalie to practice tip-ins.

Description:

Two (2) players are in front of the goal. X_1 carries the puck, and X_2 moves toward goal in the direction of the far goal post. X_1 has the option of shooting to keep the goalie honest. X_1's purpose is to get the puck to X_2 for an in tight shot or tip-in and force the goalie to react quickly for such s shot.

Participation:

Goalie, two (2) players.

Drill 141. *Shots 5*

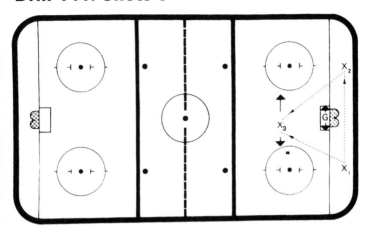

Purpose:

To provide a drill to train the goalie for shots in the slot when the opposition has the puck control behind the net.

Description:

Three (3) players are in a triangle with X_1 and X_2 behind the net and X_3 in the slot. X_1 and X_2 pass the puck between themselves and to X_3 who shoots. X_3 also moves around in the slot to position himself with the puck behind the net.

Participation:

Goalie, three (3) players.

Drill 142. Shots 6

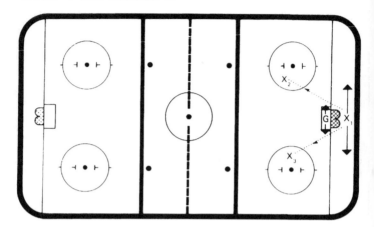

Purpose:

To provide a drill to train the goalie for shots in the slot when the opposition has puck control behind the net.

Description:

Three (3) players are in a triangle with X_1 behind the net and X_2 and X_3 in the slot. X_1 moves behind the net and passes the puck to the shooters. The shooters have the option of shooting or passing back to X_1.

Participation:

Goalie, three (3) players.

Drill 143. *Shots 7*

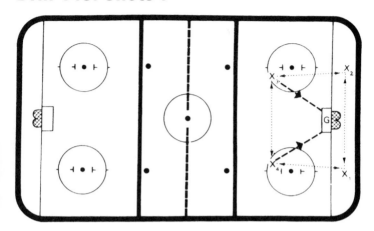

Purpose:

To provide a drill to train the goalie for shots in the slot when the opposition has puck control behind the net.

Description:

Four (4) players are in a box with X_1 and X_2 behind the net and X_3 and X_4 in the slot. X_1 and X_2 pass the puck between themselves and to X_3 and X_4. X_3 and X_4 have the options of shooting, passing between themselves, and passing back to X_1 and X_2.

Participation:

Goalie, four (4) players.

Drill 144. *Shots 8*

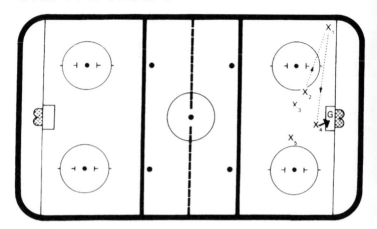

Purpose:

To provide a drill to train the goalie for shots in the slot
when the opposition has puck control in the corner.

Description:

One (1) player, X_1, is in the corner and the other players
are scattered in the slot area. X_1 passes to the other
players who shoot. Passes can be either to a set order of
players or randomly.

Participation:

Goalie, four (4) to eight (8) players.

Drill 145. *Shots 9*

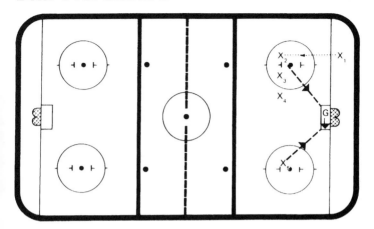

Purpose:

To provide a drill to train the goalie for shots and rebounds in the slot when the other team has puck control deep in the zone.

Description:

Performed with a number (4-8) players. One player, X_1, passes the pucks out from behind the goal line to a group of players. Another player, X_5, is off to the side with some pucks. He shoots quickly after each shot, forcing the goalie to play his shots like rebound shots.

Participation:

Goalie, number of players.

Drill 146. *Shots 10*

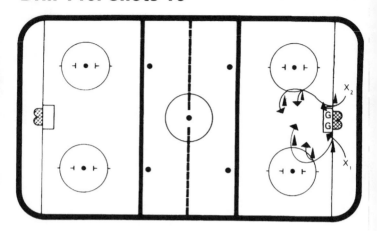

Purpose:

To provide a drill to train the goalie to stop a player coming from deep in the zone or behind the net.

Description:

Obstacles are laid out to set patterns for the player to come from deep toward the goal. The player can either attempt to jam the puck or move for a shot. Drill should have two (2) players, one from each side as shooters.

Participation:

Goalie, two (2) players.

Drill 147. *Shots 11*

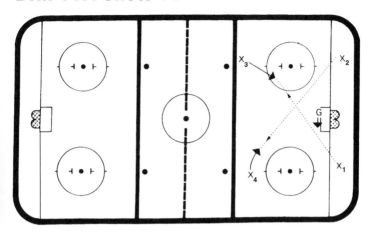

Purpose:

To provide a drill to train the goalie for shots on the pass.

Description:

Two (2) players, X_1 and X_2, are behind the goal line and two (2) players, X_3 and X_4, are near the blue line. The players deep are the passers, and the others are the shooters. X_1 passes to X_3, and X_2 passes to X_4. The shooters move toward the net and shoot on the pass.

Participation:

Goalie, four (4) players.

Drill 148. *Shots 12*

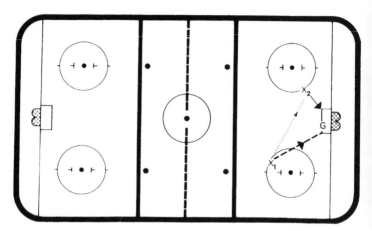

Purpose:

To provide a drill for the goalie to make saves with an offensive player at the edge of the crease.

Description:

Two (2) players are in front of the net, X_1 is out and X_2 is at the edge of the crease. X_1 shoots. X_2 moves to act as a screen for a tip-in, or a rebound.

Participation:

Goalie, two (2) players.

Drill 149. *Shots 13*

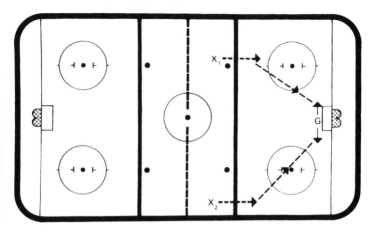

Purpose:

To provide a drill for the goalie to stop wide angle shots.

Description:

Two (2) players are wide, one on each side. They skate in alternately, taking wide shots. Drill forces the goalie to move quickly, side to side, to make the saves, working on his angles.

Participation:

Goalie, two (2) groups of players.

Drill 150. *Deflect the Pass*

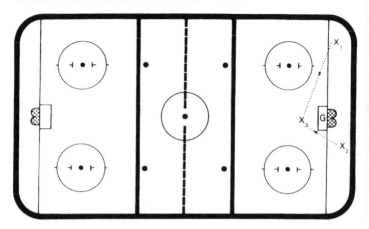

Purpose:

To provide a drill to train the goalie to deflect passes to man in the slot.

Description:

Three (3) players are involved with two (2) in deep in the zone and one (1) near the crease. The deep players make passes to the man near the crease, and the goalie deflects the passes.

Participation:

Goalie, three (3) players.

CHAPTER 7

Checking

"Over the years, I have become convinced that every detail is important and that success usually accompanies attention to little details. It is this, in my judgement, that makes for the difference between champion and near champion."

John Wooden
They Call Me Coach

Drill 151. *Forechecking 1*

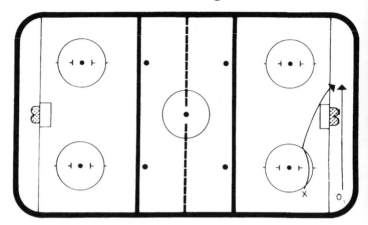

Purpose:
To provide a drill to teach the forwards to check the puckcarrier.

Description:
An offensive player (O_1) carries the puck behind the goal line. The checking forward (X) skates parallel to O_1 staying a half-stride behind while maintaining the same speed. X forces O_1 to go behind the net, prevents him from cutting up the middle, and is in a position to skate X into the boards and to maintain physical control.

Participation:
Two (2) players. Drill can be executed at both ends.

Drill 152. *Forechecking 2*

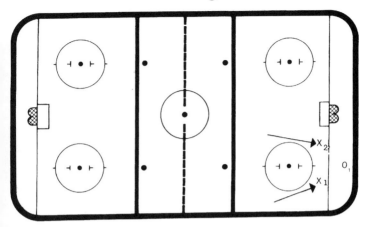

Purpose:

To provide a drill to teach two (2) forwards to pressure the puckcarrier.

Description:

The puckcarrier (O_1) starts a few feet ahead of the first forechecker (X_1). X_1 forces O_1 to the boards and in the direction of the net. The second forechecker (X_2) moves in from a different direction. The first forechecker should play the man, and the second takes the puck.

Participation:

Three (3) players. Drill can be executed at both ends.

Drill 153. *Forechecking 3*

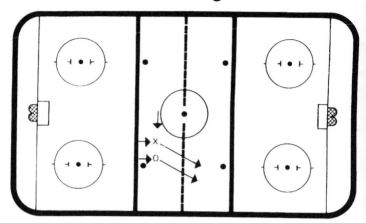

Purpose:

To provide a drill to teach 1 on 1 forechecking in the neutral zone.

Description:

An offensive player (O) skates up the ice with a puck. The forechecker (X) moves to the puckcarrier. He must not overly commit himself and be beaten. His objective is to force the player either toward or to pass to a player who is already in check (toward the boards in this drill). The forechecker should always play the man after the puck has been passed.

Participation:

Two (2) players. Drill can be executed on both sides in the neutral zone.

Drill 154. *Forechecking 4*

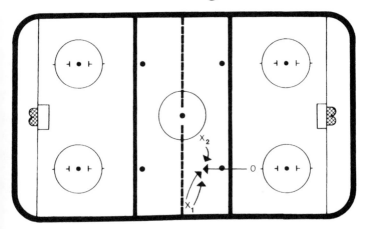

Purpose:

To provide a drill to teach the center and puckside wing to forecheck as a tandem in the neutral zone.

Description:

An offensive player (O_1) moves up the ice with the puck. The center (X_2) pressures O_1, toward the puckside wing (X_1) who can then double team the puckcarrier. X_1 and X_2 can also practice interchanging with the center going to the boards and the wing pressuring O_1.

Participation:

Three (3) players.

Drill 155. *Wings Check in Neutral Zone*

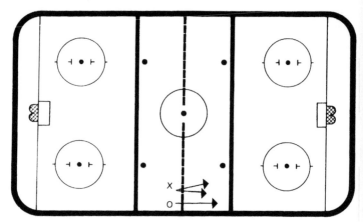

Purpose:

To provide a drill to teach the wings close checking in the neutral zone.

Description:

An offensive forward (O) without the puck skates along the boards in the neutral zone. The defensive forward (X) stays close to O preventing him from getting ahead or cutting to the middle. The checker (X) is allowed to use his body to prevent O from cutting to the middle.

Participation:

Two (2) players. Drill can be executed on both sides in the neutral zone.

Drill 156. *Defenseman 1*

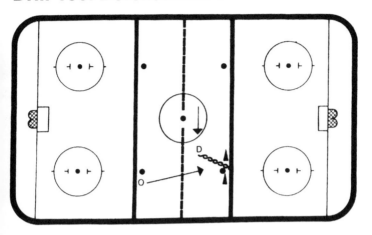

Purpose:

To provide a drill to teach the defensemen to play the man in open ice.

Description:

Two obstacles are placed in the neutral zone to restrict the offensive forward's (O) mobility. O carries the puck up the ice and the defenseman (D) makes his play by the blue line. O, staying within the obstacles, attempts to beat the defenseman or dump the puck. If O dumps the puck, D plays the man.

Participation:

Two (2) players, a defenseman and a forward.

Drill 157. *Defenseman 2*

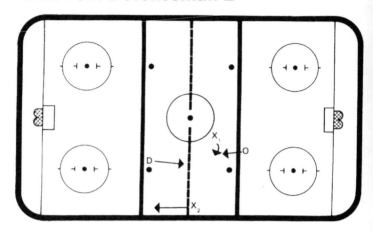

Purpose:

To provide a drill to teach the defensemen to stand up in the neutral zone.

Description:

This drill is similar to Drill 154 with a defenseman added. The puckside defenseman (D) stands up at the red line to play the puckcarrier (O) who is being pressured by the center (X_1). X_2 backchecks and covers for D.

Participation:

Four (4) players, one (1) offensive player, two (2) defensive forwards, one (1) defenseman.

Drill 158. *Defenseman 3*

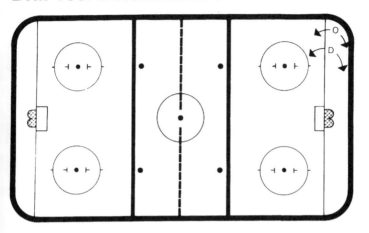

Purpose:

To provide a drill to teach the defensemen to play the man in the defensive zone.

Description:

An offensive player (O) attempts to walk out of the corner with the puck. The defenseman (D) plays the man by keeping O to the outside and keeping himself between the puck and the net. D plays O, separating him from the puck.

Participation:

Two (2) players, a forward and a defenseman.

Drill 159. *Defenseman 4*

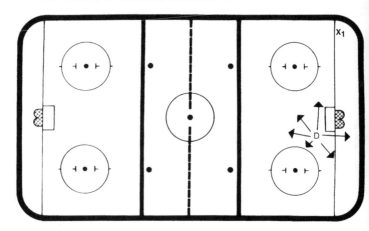

Purpose:

To provide a drill to teach the defensemen proper positioning in front of the net.

Description:

The defenseman (D) lines up on the far goal post. X_1 has the puck. This permits him to view the entire puckside area and not allow anyone to get behind him to the net. This positioning allows D to move to the opposition or to the puck.

Participation:

One (1) player, a defenseman.

Drill 160. *Center*

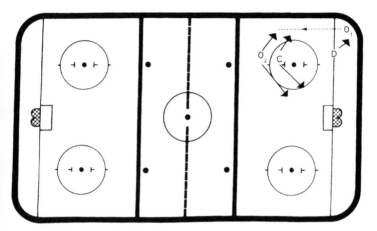

Purpose:

To provide a drill to teach the center to defense the slot area.

Description:

The center (C) stays with an offensive player (O_2) in the slot area. A second offensive player (O_1) is in the corner with a puck. A defenseman (D) plays O_1. O_1 attempts to pass to O_2 and the center must keep O_2 in check.

Participation:

Four (4) players, two (2) offensive players, one (1) defenseman, and one (1) defensive forward.

Drill 161. *Wings*

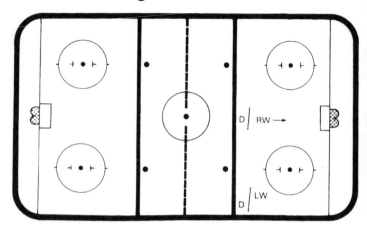

Purpose:

To provide a drill to teach the wings proper position covering the points.

Description:

This drill teaches the puckside wing to cover his point closely and the off-side wing to cover both the high slot and his point. The pointmen can move around to force the wings to adjust. Also, a player in the corner can attempt to pass to the pointmen with the wings adjusting.

Participation:

Two (2) offensive defensemen and two (2) defensive wings. Option of inserting an offensive forward with the puck.

Drill 162. *Play the Man 1*

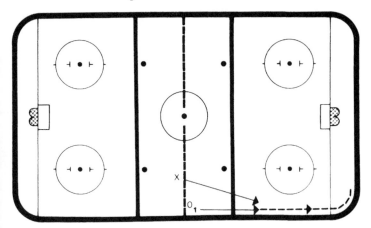

Purpose:
To provide a drill to teach the forwards to play the man.

Description:
An offensive player (O_1) skates along the boards and dumps the puck in. A defensive forward (X) takes O_1 into the boards, either before or after O_1 dumps the puck in.

Participation:
Two (2) forwards, a defensive and an offensive player.

Drill 163. *Play the Man 2*

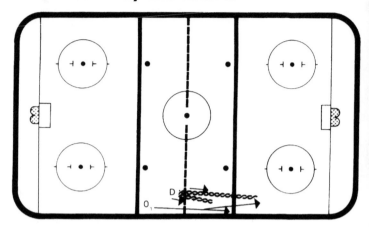

Purpose:
To provide a drill to teach the defensemen to play the offensive forward after he dumps the puck.

Description:
An offensive forward (O_1) skates along the boards and dumps the puck in. A defenseman (D), skating backwards, plays O_1 by not letting him get by and skating him into the boards.

Participation:
Two (2) players, an offensive forward and a defenseman.

Drill 164. *Play the Man 3*

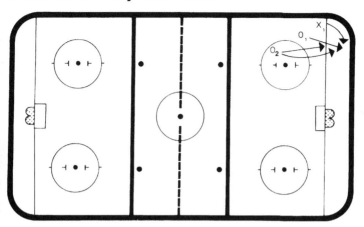

Purpose:
To provide a drill to teach the offensive forwards to play the man in the offensive zone.

Description:
A defensive player (X), who can be either a forward or a defenseman, has the puck. Two (2) offensive forwards O_1 and O_2 converge on X. O_1 plays the man and O_2 takes the puck.

Participation:
Three (3) players, a defensive player and two (2) offensive players.

Drill 165. *Play the Man 4*

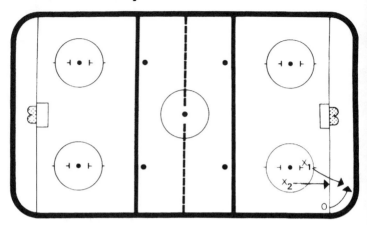

Purpose:

To provide a drill to teach the defensive players to play the man when the offensive player is deep in the zone.

Description:

An offensive player (O) has the puck deep in the offensive zone and is carrying the puck. The first defensive player (X_1) normally, but not always a defenseman, plays the man; and the second defensive player (X_2) takes the puck.

Participation:

Three (3) players, an offensive player and two (2) defensive players.

Drill 166. *Play the Man 5*

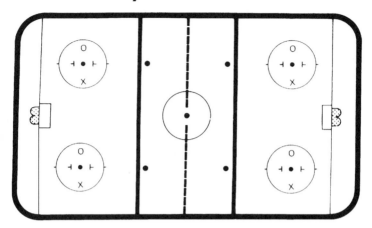

Purpose:

To provide a drill to teach playing the man in open space.

Description:

Two (2) players, an offensive (O) and a defensive (X) player are inside the face-off circle. Within the confines of the circle, O tries to get by X. Sticks and puck are optional. Drill can also be executed with two (2) defensive players and one (1) offensive player.

Participation:

Two (2) or three players, an offensive player and one (1) or two (2) defensive players.

Drill 167. *Play the Man 6*

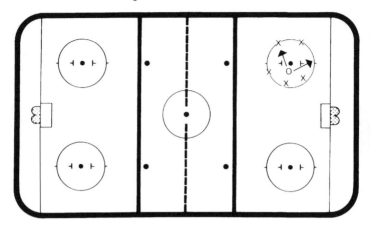

Purpose:
To provide a drill to teach playing the man in open space.

Description:
An offensive player (O) is in the middle of a face-off circle, and a number of defensive players (X) are on the face-off circle edge. O tries to beat the X's and get outside the circle. Sticks and puck are optional.

Participation:
One (1) offensive player and four (4) to six (6) defensive players to each circle.

Drill 168. *Play the Man 7*

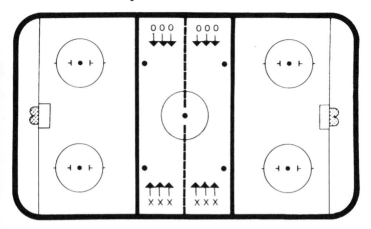

Purpose:

To provide a drill to teach playing the man in open spaces.

Description:

Performed with two (2) groups of players: offensive (O) with the pucks and defensive (X). Each group is on opposite boards. They skate towards each other. The O's try to beat the X's and the X's (without sticks) attempt to bodycheck the O's.

Participation:

The entire team, two (2) groups.

Drill 169. *Blocking Passes*

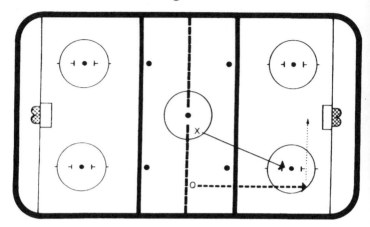

Purpose:

To provide a drill to teach the defensive players to make a "last ditch" save of a pass.

Description:

An offensive player (O) carries the puck down the ice close to the boards. A defensive player, coming from behind, dives to block a pass from O. A second offensive player can be inserted to receive the attempted pass.

Participation:

One (1) defensive player and one (1) or two (2) offensive players.

Variations:

The defensive forward will start like a late backchecker and try to get back into the play. The defenseman should start by skating backwards and turns, skates forward, and dives to block pass.

Drill 170. *Play the Man 9*

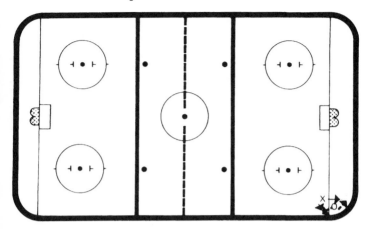

Purpose:

To provide a drill to teach the defensive player to freeze the puck in the defensive zone.

Description:

Two players fight for the puck along the boards. The offensive player (O) attempts to free the puck and the defensive player (X) attempts to freeze the puck and control O.

Participation:

Two (2) players, an offensive and defensive puck.

Drill 171. *Play the Man 10*

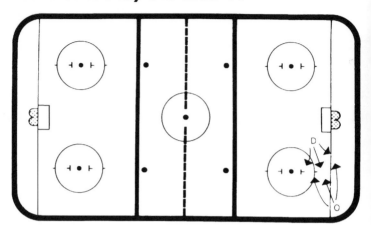

Purpose:

To provide a drill to teach the defensemen to play the man coming from the corner toward the net.

Description:

An offensive player (O) with a puck comes from the corner or deep in the zone. The defenseman (D) picks up O and prevents him from getting to the net area.

Participation:

Two (2) players, an offensive and a defensive player.

Drill 172.

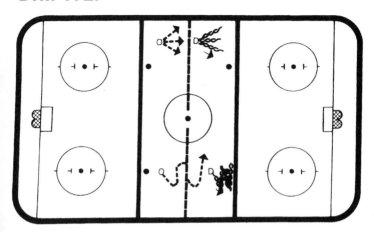

Purpose:
To provide a drill to teach the defenseman to play the man in the neutral zone.

Description:
An offensive player (O) skates through the neutral zone with the puck. He may go in any direction or skate in a tight weave pattern. The defenseman (D) skates backwards, prevents O from getting by, and, if possible, to bodycheck O off the puck.

Participation:
One (1) offensive player and one (1) defenseman.

Drill 173. *Blocking Shots*

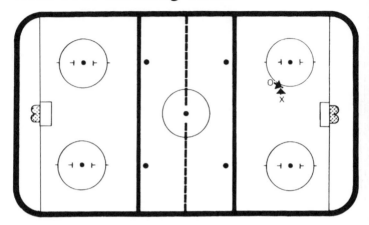

Purpose:

To provide a drill to teach the defenseman to block shots.

Description:

Using tennis balls, an offensive player (O) takes shots. The defensive player (X) blocks the shots. Practice the different blocks, dropping to both knees, sliding with the body, standing erect with feet together and the toes of both skates pointing directly at the shooter.

Participation:

Two (2) players, an offensive player and a defensive player.

Drill 174. *Bumping*

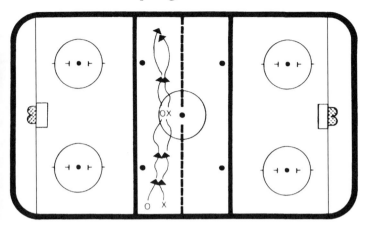

Purpose:

To provide a drill to teach constant contact and strength for contact.

Description:

Performed with players in pairs. Start with no pucks and no sticks, progress to the O's with the pucks and X's with no sticks, and then X's with sticks. Players simply bump each other at close quarters.

Participation:

The entire team divided into pairs.

Drill 175. *Play the Man 12*

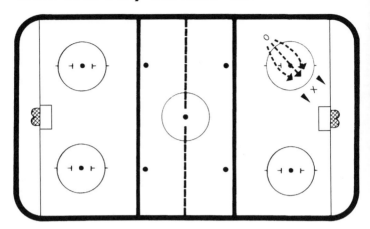

Purpose:
To provide a drill to teach the defensemen to play the man close to the net and prevent a shot on goal.

Description:
Two (2) obstacles are laid out. The defenseman (D) starts between the two obstacles. The offensive player (O) must skate between the obstacles and deke D and get a shot off. D must play O and prevent him from shooting.

Participation:
Two (2) players, an offensive player and a defenseman.

CHAPTER 8

Situations

"Today's hockey player should be fully aware that it is not the man in possession but the players moving into the open spaces that give any combined movement its impetus."

Horst Wein
The Science of Hockey

Drill 176. *1-1/2-1. 1*

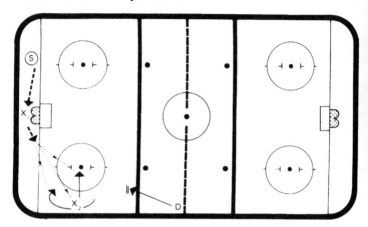

Purpose:

To provide a drill for 1-1 and 2-1's with a breakout pass.

Description:

Performed with two (2) offensive players and one (1) defenseman. X_1 makes a breakout pass to X_2 who is on the boards. X_2 has a number of options to choose the direction he wants to go. The defenseman (D) moves up from the red line to play X_2 on the 1-1. To make drill a 2-1, insert a second forward.

Tempo:

Drill is executed at full speed.

Participation:

Two (2) offensive players for 1-1, three (3) for 2-1, and one (1) defenseman. Drill can be worked from both ends alternately.

Variations:

Another offensive player can be added to allow for a second pass to be made prior to the breakout.

Drill 177. *1-1/2-1. 2*

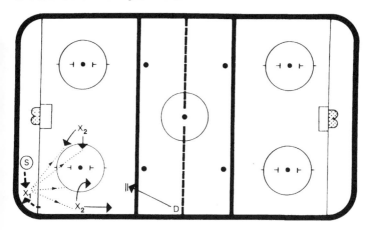

Purpose:
To provide a drill for 1-1 and 2-1's with a breakout pass.

Description:
Performed with two (2) offensive players and one (1) defenseman. X_1 makes a breakout pass to X_2 who is in the middle. X_2 has a number of options to choose the direction he wants to go. The defenseman (D) moves up from the red line to play X_2 on the 1-1. To make the drill a 2-1, insert a second forward.

Tempo:
Drill is executed at full speed.

Participation:
Two (2) offensive players for 1-1, three (3) for 2-1 and one (1) defenseman. Drill can be worked from both ends alternately.

Variations:
Another offensive player can be added to allow for a second pass to be made prior to the breakout.

Drill 178. *1-1/2-1. 3*

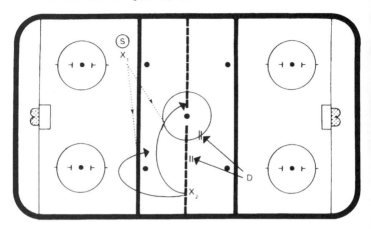

Purpose:

To provide a drill for 1-1 and 2-1's with an outlet pass in the neutral zone.

Description:

Performed with two (2) offensive players and one (1) defenseman. X_1, from his blue line area, makes an outlet pass to X_2 who is coming off the boards. The defenseman (D) moves up from inside his blue line to play X_2 on the 1-1. To make the drill a 2-1, insert a second forward.

Tempo:

Drill is executed at full speed.

Participation:

Two (2) offensive players for 1-1, three (3) for 2-1 and one (1) defenseman. Drill can be worked in both directions.

Variations:

Another offensive player can be added to allow for a second pass to be made prior to the breakout.

Drill 179. *1-1/2-1. 4*

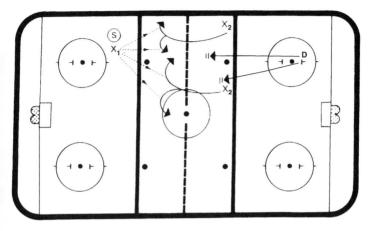

Purpose:
To provide a drill for 1-1 and 2-1's with an outlet pass in the neutral zone.

Description:
Performed with two (2) offensive players and one (1) defenseman. X_1, from his blue line area, makes an outlet pass to X_2 who is coming back up the middle or off the boards close to X_1. The defenseman (D) moves up from inside his blue line to play X_2 on the 1-1. To make the drill a 2-1, insert a second forward.

Tempo:
Drill is executed at full speed.

Participation:
Two (2) offensive players for 1-1, three (3) for 2-1 and one (1) defenseman. Drill can be worked in both directions.

Variations:
Another offensive player can be added to allow for a second pass to be made prior to the breakout.

Drill 180. *1-1/2-1.* 5

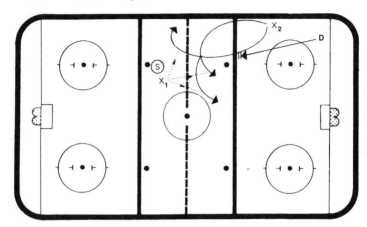

Purpose:

To provide a drill for 1-1 and 2-1's with an outlet pass in the neutral zone.

Description:

Performed with two (2) offensive players and one (1) defenseman. X_1, from the red line area, makes an outlet pass to X_2 who is just coming over the blue line. The defenseman (D) moves up from deep in his zone to play X_2 on the 1-1. To make the drill a 2-1, insert a second forward.

Tempo:

Drill is executed at full speed.

Participation:

Two (2) offensive players for 1-1, three (3) for 2-1 and one (1) defenseman. Drill can be worked in both directions.

Variations:

Another offensive player can be added to allow for a second pass to be made prior to the breakout.

Drill 181. *3-2/3-1. 1*

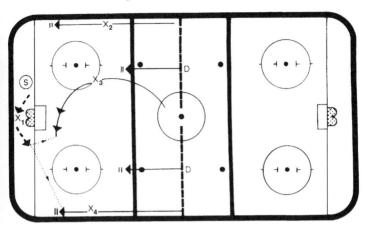

Purpose:

To provide a drill for 3-2 and 3-1's with a breakout pass.

Description:

Performed with four (4) offensive players and two (2) defensemen. X_1 makes a breakout pass to X_2, X_2, X_3, or X_4. The defensemen (D) move up from the red line to play the 3-2. To make drill 3-1, use only one (1) defenseman.

Tempo:

Drill is executed at full speed.

Participation:

Four (4) offensive players and two (2) defensemen for 3-2 and one (1) defenseman for 3-1. Drill can be worked in both directions.

Variations:

Another offensive player can be added to allow for a second pass to be made prior to the breakout. Insert a defensive forward for a 3-3 drill.

Drill 182. *3-2/3-1. 2*

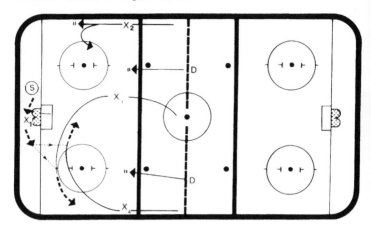

Purpose:

To provide a drill for 3-2 and 3-1's with a breakout pass.

Description:

Performed with four (4) offensive players and two (2) defensemen. X_1 makes a breakout pass to either X_3 or X_4 who crisscross in their own end. The defensemen (D) move up from the red line. To make drill 3-1, use only one (1) defenseman.

Tempo:

Drill is executed at full speed.

Participation:

Four (4) offensive players and two (2) defensemen for 3-2 and one (1) defenseman for 3-1. Drill can be worked both ways.

Variations:

Another offensive player can be added to allow for a second pass to be made prior to the breakout. Insert a defensive forward for a 3-3 drill.

Drill 183. *3-2/3-1. 3*

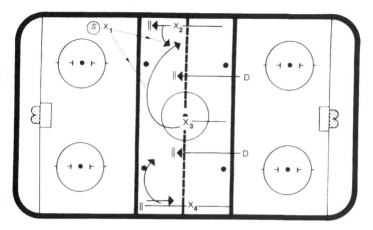

Purpose:

To provide a drill for 3-2 and 3-1's with an outlet pass in the neutral zone.

Description:

Performed with four (4) offensive players and two (2) defensemen. X_1, from his blue line area, makes an outlet pass to X_2, X_3, or X_4 in the neutral zone. The defensemen (D) move up from inside their blue line to play the 3-2. To make drill 3-1, use only one (1) defenseman.

Tempo:

Drill is executed at full speed.

Participation:

Four (4) offensive players and two (2) defensemen for 3-2 and one (1) defenseman for 3-1. Drill can be worked in both directions.

Variations:

Another offensive player can be added to allow for a second pass to be made prior to the breakout. Insert a defensive forward for a 3-3 drill.

Drill 184. *3-2/3-1. 4*

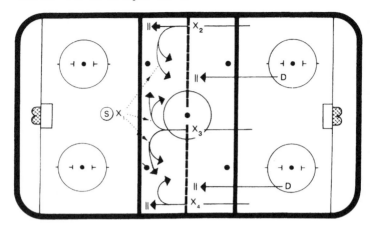

Purpose:

To provide a drill for 3-2 and 3-1's with an outlet pass in the neutral zone.

Description:

Performed with four (4) offensive players and two (2) defensemen. X_1, from his blue line area, makes an outlet pass to X_2, X_3, or X_4 in the neutral zone. The defensemen (D) move up from inside their blue line to play the 3-2. To make drill 3-1, use only one (1) defenseman.

Tempo:

Drill is executed at full speed.

Participation:

Four (4) offensive players and two (2) defensemen for 3-2 and one (1) defenseman for 3-1. Drill can be worked in both directions.

Variations:

Another offensive player can be added to allow for a second pass to be made prior to the breakout. Insert a defensive forward for a 3-3 drill.

Drill 185. *3-2/3-1.5*

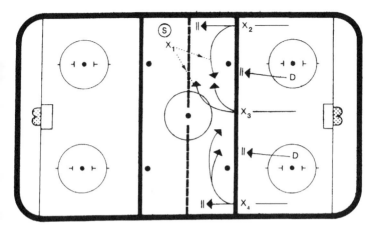

Purpose:
To provide a drill for 3-2 and 3-1's with an outlet pass in the neutral zone.

Description:
Performed with four (4) offensive players and two (2) defensemen. X_1, from the red line area, makes an outlet pass to X_2, X_3, or X_4 who are coming over the blue line. The defensemen (D) move up from deep in their zone to play the 3-2. To make drill 3-1, use only one (1) defenseman.

Tempo:
Drill is executed at full speed.

Participation:
Four (4) offensive players and two (2) defensemen for 3-2 and one (1) defenseman for 3-1. Drill can be worked in both directions.

Variations:
Another offensive player can be added to allow for a second pass to be made prior to the breakout. Insert a defensive forward for 3-3 drill.

Drill 186. *Fastbreak 1*

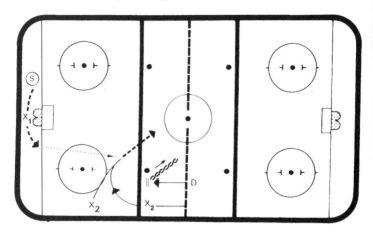

Purpose:
To provide a drill for a fastbreak from the defensive zone.

Description:
Performed with two (2) offensive players and one (1) defenseman. X_1, from deep in his zone, makes a pass up the middle to X_2 who is breaking up the middle. The defenseman (D) moves in from the red line.

Tempo:
Drill is executed at full speed.

Participation:
Two (2) offensive players and one (1) defenseman.

Variations:
Additional offensive players can be inserted to make the breakout multiple player.

Drill 187. *Fastbreak 2*

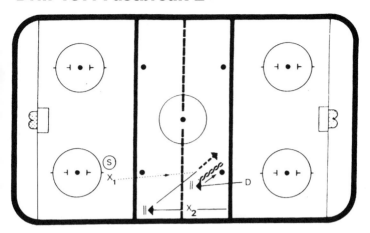

Purpose:

To provide a drill for a fastbreak from the neutral zone.

Description:

Performed with two (2) offensive players and one (1) defenseman. X_1, from near in his blue line, passes up the middle to X_2 who moves through the middle. The defenseman (D) moves up from his zone.

Tempo:

Drill is executed at full speed.

Participation:

Two (2) offensive players and one (1) defenseman.

Variations:

Additional offensive players can be inserted to make the breakout multiple player.

Drill 188. *Continuous 3-2*

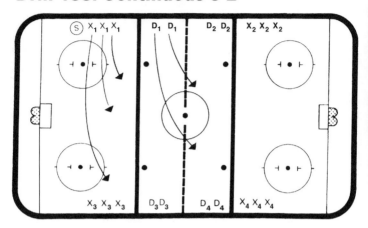

Purpose:

To provide a drill for 3-2 with constant movement.

Description:

Forwards are divided into groups of three (3).
Defensemen are divided into pairs. The first group, X_1's,
start drill with a rush. When they pass the blue line, the
second group, X_2's, start a rush the other way. Defensive
pairs react accordingly.

Tempo:

Drill is executed at full speed.

Participation:

The entire team.

Drill 189. *1-1 Both Ways*

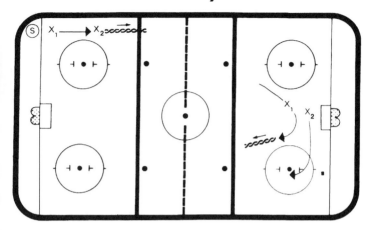

Purpose:
To provide a drill for 1-1 with constant movement.

Description:
Performed with two (2) players making 1-1 rush. After first rush, they switch roles and make a 1-1 rush the other way.

Tempo:
Drill is executed at full speed.

Participation:
The entire team. Up to four (4) rushes can be in progress simultaneously.

Variations:
Insert a third player for 2-1 drill.

Drill 190. *2-1 With Backchecker Both Ways*

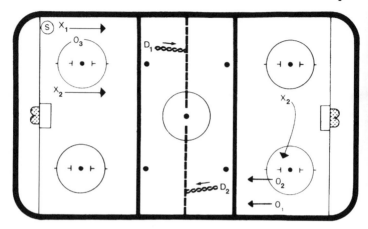

Purpose:

To provide a drill for a 2-1 drill which an offensive forward has to make the transition to defense.

Description:

Two (2) forwards, X_1 and X_2, make a rush against O_3, the backchecker, and D_1, the defenseman. One of the forwards, X_2, becomes the backchecker in a 2-1 rush the other way led by O_2 and O_1.

Tempo:

Drill is executed at full speed.

Participation:

The entire team.

Variations:

D1 can make the breakout pass for the second rush.

Drill 191. *2-1 Both Ways*

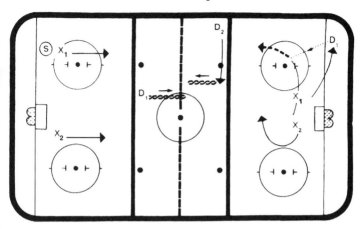

Purpose:

To provide a 2-1 drill that has the forwards make two (2) rushes.

Description:

Two (2) forwards (X_1 and X_2) make a 2-1 rush against the defenseman (D_1). A second rush is made the other way with D_1 making the breakout pass with D_2 the defenseman. D_2 would make the breakout pass for the next rush.

Tempo:

Drill is executed at full speed.

Participation:

The entire team.

Drill 192. *2-1/3-1 With Backchecker*

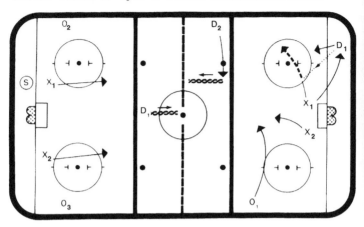

Purpose:

To provide a 2-1/3-1 drill with a backchecker.

Description:

This drill is the same as Drill 191 with the addition of a backchecker. The backchecker (O_1) picks up one of the forwards. A third forward added makes it a 3-1 drill with a backchecker.

Tempo:

Drill is executed at full speed.

Participation:

The entire team.

Drill 193. *3-2 Both Ways*

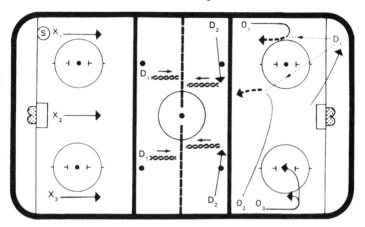

Purpose:

To provide a 3-2 drill with constant motion both ways.

Description:

Three (3) forwards (X_1, X_2, and X_3) make a rush against the defensive pair (D_1's). At the completion of the rush, one of the defensemen (D_1) makes the breakout pass for the second group of forwards (O_1, O_2, and O_3). Another defensive pair (D_2's) are in the second rush.

Tempo:

Drill is executed at full speed.

Participation:

The entire team.

Drill 194. *3-2/4-1*

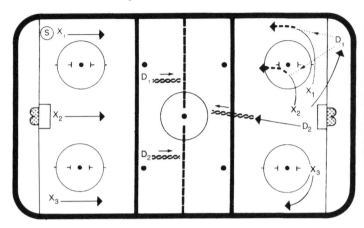

Purpose:

To provide a transition drill for the defensemen in a 3-2/4-1 rush.

Description:

Performed with three (3) forwards, X_1, X_2, and X_3, making a rush against two (2) defensemen (D_1 and D_2). After the initial rush, D_1 makes the breakout pass to the X's and joins them in a 4-1 rush against the other defenseman (D_2).

Tempo:

Drill is executed at full speed.

Participation:

The entire team.

Variations:

Add a defensive forward to make drill 3-3/4-2.

Drill 195. *3-2/5-2*

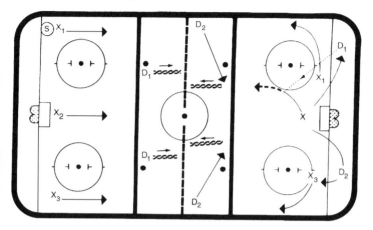

Purpose:

To provide a drill for 3-2/5-2 with constant movement.

Description:

Performed with three (3) forwards, X_1, X_2, and X_3, making a 3-2 rush against the defensive pair (D_1's). After the initial rush, a second rush is made 5-2 with the D_1's with the X's against the defensive pair (D_2's). D_1 makes the outlet pass on 5-2.

Tempo:

Drill is executed at full speed.

Participation:

The entire team.

Variations:

Add a defensive forward to make drill 3-3/5-3.

Drill 196. *1-1 Game*

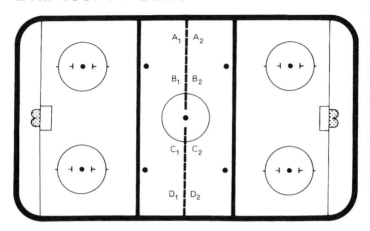

Purpose:

To provide a drill for a competitive game.

Description:

Multiple pairs are on the ice. Each pair plays a 1-1 game, i.e., A_1 vs. A_2. Winners play against winners.

Tempo:

Drill is executed at full speed.

Participation:

The entire team, up to five (5) games of 1-1 can be played simultaneously.

Drill 197. *Empty Net Game*

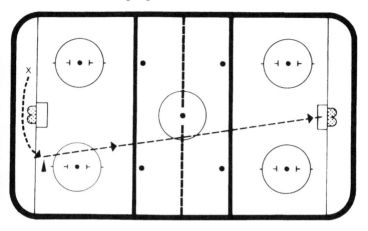

Purpose:

To provide a drill for a relaxed game.

Description:

Players skate around the net and shoot the puck at the empty net at the other end. Puck must be shot before shooter gets to face-off circle. Game continues until only one (1) player is left.

Tempo:

Drill is executed at 3/4 speed.

Participation:

The entire team.

Drill 198. *Games of 3-3*

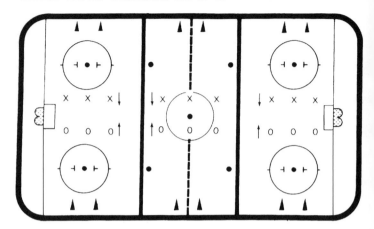

Purpose:
To provide a drill for a competitive game of 3-3.

Description:
Teams of three (3) players play against each other.
Games are played in all three zones. This means that up to 18 players can play simultaneously.

Tempo:
Drill is executed at 3/4 to full speed.

Participation:
The entire team.

Drill 199. *Games of 4-4*

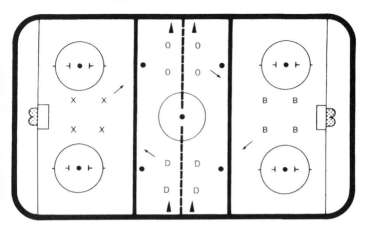

Purpose:

To provide a drill for a competitive game of 4-4.

Description:

Team is divided into groups of four (4). Each team, X's, O's, B's, and D's, have a goal to defend and a goal to score in. This means 16 players can play simultaneously.

Tempo:

Drill is executed at 3/4 to full speed.

Participation:

The entire team.

Drill 200. *Full Squad Game*

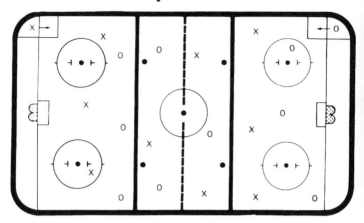

Purpose:

To provide a drill for a competitive game utilizing the entire team.

Description:

Team is divided into two squads, X's and O's. Each team has defenders, mid-fielders, and scorers. The players cannot leave their appropriate zones. The puck has to move from zone to zone, i.e., defenders to mid-fielders to scorers. Keep score.

Tempo:

Drill is executed at full speed.

Participation:

The entire team.

Variations:

Have up to three pucks in play at once.

CHAPTER 9

Practice

"Every drill has its purpose. Not only are they devised to improve general condition, but also improve some basic fundamentals of the game."

John Wooden
They Call Me Coach

"The results of training depend on good organization. However, to no less degree do they depend on the proper methods which the coach employs, not only in selecting, but also conducting each drill or lesson on the whole."

Anatoli Tarasov
The Road To Olympus

A good hockey team will be a good practice team. The same for a coach and the coaching staff. A good game coach needs to be a good practice coach. The coaching staff must put both time and effort into the practices for them to be fruitful.

Every coach must ask himself "How can I get the maximum use of the facility with the maximum amount of participation of the players to accomplish the objectives of the practice?" This question can only be answered and then implemented by putting time and effort into the design of the practice.

Coaches should not hesitate to use new and innovative ideas in their practices. Other sports can provide different ideas that are counter but productive, to the traditional North American methods. Practices should not be with one coach, a lot of scrimmaging, a few drills and plenty of ice not being utilized.

Here are some suggestions to be considered when planning practices:

1. The one coach system should, if possible be abandoned. It is not possible for one coach to effectively train, develop and teach 15-22 players simultaneously on the ice.
2. Define the objectives of each practice: what should be accomplished in the areas of skills, conditioning and tactics.
3. What are the capabilities of the players? The content of the practices need to complement their ability levels.
4. Decide how best to implement the objectives: what drills are to be used, how much time, if any, should be spent scrimmaging, and how should the conditioning aspect be accomplished.
5. Specify how much time is to be spent on each part of practice. Once the time specifics are determined, they should be maintained.
6. Following each practice, the coaches should review the practice, evaluate its strengths and weaknesses, and

make suggestions on how to make improvements for future practices
7. Keep practices from being boring. Boredom creates a non-learning atmosphere.
8. Keep a record of all practices. They will be useful for future references.

Year Long Plan

The coaching staff needs to have an idea of what has to be accomplished over the year. Prior to the start of the season, a year (season) long plan should be completed. This plan should outline the development of the team and its individual members for the year.

What should be included in the year long plan? First, the progress of the team, both technically and tactically, needs to be projected. Where should the team be at specific dates are the guidelines. This, in part, determines the approach to teaching the team's systems. It also determines the types of drills used and which skills to emphasize at different times. The plan helps the coaching staff stay calm and focused when things, i.e., team is in a slump, are not going well. Second, how the progress of the individual players is to be monitored is established. The plan takes into consideration the development of skills, how to improve the players' weaknesses and to determine both the team's and the individual's progress.

Drill Selection

1. Select drills that complement the team's level of ability. Do not use drills that are too difficult or complex for the team's present ability level.
2. Select drills that utilize the entire, or as near as possible, ice surface. This can be done with one or a group of drills being executed at different spots simultaneously.
3. Select drills that utilize as many players as possible. It is important to keep the players active throughout the practice.

4. Select drills that complement the team's system of play.
5. The time span of a specific drill should not be too long which often leads to boredom or too short to successfully accomplish the drill's purpose.
6. All drills are fundamental. Keep in mind that drills to teach the basic fundamentals are always useful. No team ever progresses beyond the need for fundamental drills. There is no such thing as a drill being too basic or too simple.
7. Drills should be compatible to the players, coaches, and as a unit, the team.
8. Consider whether your team likes a large number or a few drills. Each team has a distinct personality. Some teams like a large number of drills. Other teams are more comfortable with only a few familiar drills.

The following example practices are comprised of four components: skills (S), tactics (T), conditioning (C) and fun competition (F). They are 60 minutes in length. They are meant to be types of practices. Any number of drills can be used within the types.

Example Practices

——————— **I** ———————

0-5 Warm-ups (S)

Light skating, doing turns, spins, falls, etc. with and without pucks.

6-15 Skill drills (S)

Three (3) drills, one (1) in each zone. (A) Backward skating on a face-off circle. (B) Players skate a figure 8 while stickhandling. (C) Standing still on a face-off circle, players make passes.

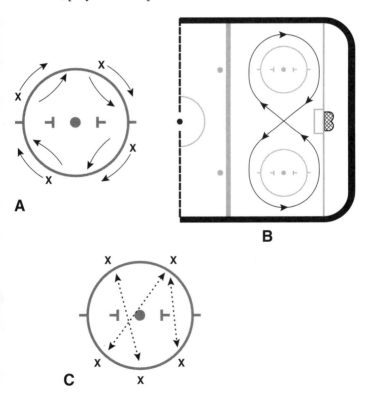

A

B

C

16-30 Breakout drills (T)

1 on 1's, 2 on 1's, 3 on 1's (2's). Defenseman begins drill with an outlet pass.

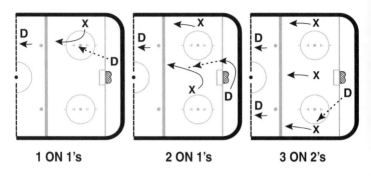

1 ON 1's **2 ON 1's** **3 ON 2's**

31-35 Conditioning drill (C)

Players skate 1-½ laps, skate 22 sec., rest 44 sec. 3 times.

36-40 Passing drill (S)

Pairs make one touch passes while moving in one (1) zone.

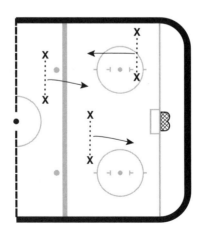

41-50 Forechecking (T)

Instruction on forechecking system and players go through it as well as possible adjustments of the opposition.

51-55 Conditioning drill (C)

Players skate hard to the blue line, turn and come back to the goal line easy. Skate 4 sec./rest 12 sec. 6-8 times.

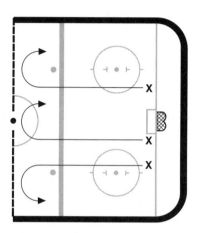

56-60 Relay race (F)

Teams of four (4) players each, down and back once.

II

0-5 Warm-ups (S)

Skating easy, players in groups of three (3) pass the puck between themselves. One (1) player skates backward, two (2) forward.

6-15 Shooting drills (S)

Two (2) shooting drills, one (1) in each end. (A) Player breaks off wing and shoots. (B) Forward passes to defenseman, breaks to the net, receives a return pass and shoots.

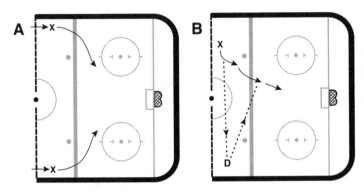

16-22 Defensive zone coverage (T)

Instruction on defensive zone coverage.

23-28 Counter-attack (T)

Three (3) forwards begin 3 on 2 attack with outlet pass from a defenseman. Drill goes both ways.

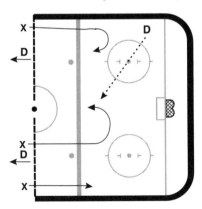

29-35 Conditioning drill (C)
Players skate down and back. Skate 15 sec./rest 45 sec.
5 times.

36-40 Stickhandling drill (S)
Players skate laps and (A) weave around cones, (B)
make circles around cones and (C) stop at cones.

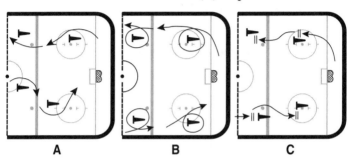

A   B   C

41-55 Power Play and Penalty Killing (T)
Instruction and execution of power play and man down
situations.

56-60 Target shooting (F)
From the blue line, players try to hit frisbee that is
hanging from the net.

0-5 Warm-ups (S)

Skating easy, in pairs, players pass the puck between themselves and then play one on one. Executed while skating laps.

6-10 Shooting drill (S)

Players swing out of the corners and shoot on the goal.

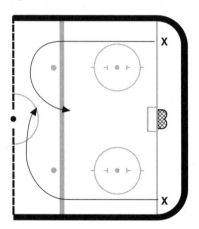

11-20 Passing drills (S)

Two (2) drills executed on face-off circle. (A) Stationary passing and (B) While skating, make pass to man ahead.

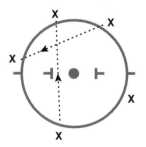 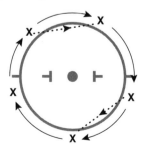

21-27 Neutralzzone counter-attack (T)
Instruction on the neutral zone counter-attack.

28-35 Conditioning drill (C)
Skate width of the ice, over and back. Skate 15 sec./rest 45 sec. 5 times.

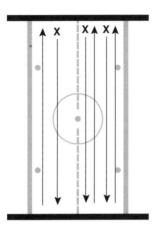

36-43 Puckhandling drill (S)
Players work on taking a pass in the feet and deflecting the puck to the stick.

44-50 Stickhandling drill (S)

Players working in pairs begin passing the puck between themselves. On whistle, they play 1 on 1 trying to keep the puck to themselves.

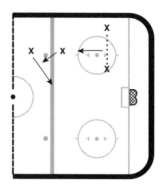

51-55 Shooting drill (S)

One (1) player moves to the corner with a puck. Second player moves to the slot area and shoots or deflects pass from the first player.

56-60 Rapid shooting (F)

Each player shoots 5 pucks quickly from the red line at the empty goal.

0-5 Warm-ups (S)

Start with light, easy skating and gradually pick up the tempo.

6-10 Stickhandling drill (S)

Players, in groups of 4 or 5, while carrying the puck, skate circles at each face-off circle.

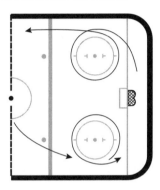

11-25 Skill drills (S)

(A) Player moves with the puck from the corner toward the net or the slot area. (B) Two (2) players skate up ice making short passes and come back wide, each carrying the puck. (C) The players each have a puck and try to avoid each other while moving in the neutral zone.

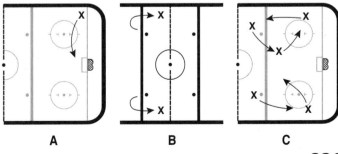

| A | B | C |

26-30 Face-offs (T)

Instructions on face-offs.

31-40 Conditioning drill (C)

Players in groups of 4 or 5, skate 2 laps.
Skate 30 sec./rest 90 sec. 4 times.

41-50 Power Play and Penalty Killing (T)

Using units, both the power play and man down
situations are practiced.

51-60 Games of 3 vs. 3 (F)

Using the width of the ice, 3 separate games of 3 vs. 3
are played. Emphasize quick, short passes.

---------------- **V** ----------------

0-5 Warm-ups (S)

Easy skating and stretching, skate three (3) laps each
at a quicker tempo.

6-15 Skating drills (S)

Two (2) drills. (A) Players skate to the red line, stop,
take 2 or 3 quick strides in the other direction. (B) Work
on forward and backward crossovers while skating on a
face-off circle.

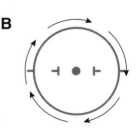

16-25 Aerobic skate (C)

Players skate at 60-70% maximum continuously in laps.
Skate 3 min./rest 1 min. 2 times.

26-40 Forechecking and breakouts (T)

Working with two (2) units in each end, practice
forechecking systems and breakout plays.

41-50 Skill drills (S)

Three (3) drills. (A) Players work on taking pass off the
boards. (B) Players work on turns by skating figure 8's
going hard on turns and easy on straightaways. (C)
Shooting drill has player receive a pass as he moves into
slot area and shoots.

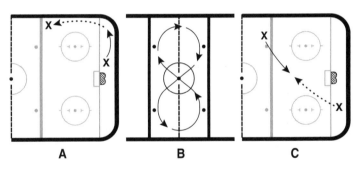

A   B   C

51-55 Conditioning drill (C)

Players work short, quick intervals by skating hard for 5
sec./rest 20 sec. while carrying a puck. 8 times.

56-60 Showdown (F)

0-5 Warm-ups (S)

Easy skating with players working in pairs shadowing each other.

6-10 Shooting drill (S)

Players come off boards and shoot.

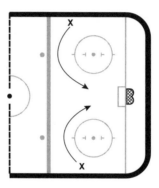

11-20 Checking (T)

(A) Centers and defensemen work on coverage in the net and the slot area. (B) Wings work on covering checks while backchecking.

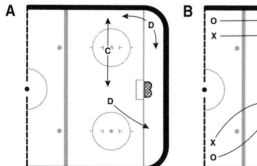
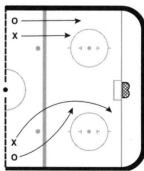

21-35 Conditioning drill (C)

Players skate three (3) laps. Skate 60 sec./rest 180 sec.
3 times.

36-46 Skating drills (S)

Two (2) skating drills. (A) Players work on stepovers
and (B) Agility training with players moving in all four
(4) directions.

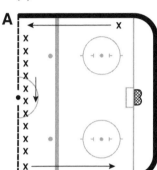

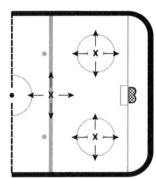

46-50 Breakout play (T)

Units breakout 5 on 2 to neutral zone, regroup and
breakout a second time. Work both ends.

51-55 Conditioning drill (C)

Players skate between red line and blue line
continuously. Skate 15 sec./rest 45 sec. 4 times.

56-60 Agility test (F)

Players are timed while skating an agility course.
(Approximately 20 sec.).